ISSUES

Alternative Texts for Advanced Students

Nelson

Phil Bowman

Thomas Nelson and Sons Ltd
Nelson House Mayfield Road
Walton-on-Thames Surrey
KT12 5PL UK

51 York Place
Edinburgh
EH1 3JD UK

Thomas Nelson (Hong Kong) Ltd
Toppan Building 10/F
22A Westlands Road
Quarry Bay Hong Kong

© P. Bowman   1989

First published by Thomas Nelson and Sons Ltd 1989

ISBN 0-17-555727-6

NPN 9 8 7 6 5 4 3 2

Printed in Great Britain by
M & A Thomson Litho Ltd.
East Kilbride, Scotland.

Contents

Introduction   4

The Social Hierarchy,
Class and Privilege
Unit 1   Monarchy—are we being brainwashed?   7
Unit 2   Democracy or a Class System?   12
Unit 3   A Sloane Ranger Speaks   16

Money
Unit 4   The Rich Kids   24
Unit 5   Value for Money?   29

Test 1   35

Sport and Leisure
Unit 6   Tennis under Threat   38
Unit 7   Clough Blasts Royal Hunters   43

Education
Unit 8   Survival of the Thickest?   50
Unit 9   Theory X versus Theory Y   56
Unit 10   Brains + Hard Work = Genius   62

Test 2   67

Social Problems
Unit 11   Playing Away   70
Unit 12   Drying Out   78
Unit 13   Smack City   84

Crime and Punishment
Unit 14   The Finger of Suspicion   90
Unit 15   It's a Steal in the City   95

Test 3   101

Work
Unit 16   Bosses v. Workers   104
Unit 17   Final Placement Syndrome   109

Men versus Women
Unit 18   A Neutered Society   115
Unit 19   Men on the Receiving End   122
Unit 20   A Female Reaction   128

Test 4   133

Communication Activities   136

Answer Key   146

Answer Key to Tests   174

Introduction

This book was written with two principal aims:
- to present topics through authentic material which will challenge and interest students sufficiently to make them want to develop their active as well as their passive skills.
- to give intensive practice in the types of question students will encounter in the Cambridge Proficiency in English and other advanced examinations, and to help students improve the related skills.

These two requirements are kept in mind throughout the book.

Students using the book should be at a level of English approximating to post-Cambridge First Certificate. Although much of the material is geared to the Proficiency examination, the choice of texts and language practice is also relevant to general advanced-level classes.

In an examination, the texts are chosen because they are suitable for testing purposes, not because they are particularly interesting. There is no reason why this principle should be extended to coursebooks—as so often seems to be the case. The texts and visual material in ISSUES have been chosen because they are likely to entertain, and, in some cases, provoke and challenge students intellectually. The material is intended to provide opportunities to get away from 'the coursebook', while at the same time linking thematically with many of the topic areas covered in advanced courses. All the material has been taken from authentic sources (novels, non-fiction books, newspapers, magazines, advertisements, letters), exposing students to a wide variety of register.

ISSUES is intended primarily for classroom use. However, with the answer key, it can also be used successfully for self-study purposes.

The Units

Design and Content
Each unit follows the same basic format. However, it is not essential to work chronologically through every unit, or, indeed, cover all the material contained in each unit. For example, much of the oral practice material could be brought forward and used as lead-in exercises. It is up to the teacher to decide what the students' needs are and what would fit in with the course objectives.

There are 20 units, each divided into three sections.

Reading comprehension
Introductory text(s) with one of the following question types:
- multiple-choice (as in Proficiency Paper 1, Section B)
- context (as in Proficiency Paper 3, Section B)
- true/false/not clear
- broken-up text to reassemble in proper sequence.
In many units there are also vocabulary exercises.

Use of English
Exercises linked structurally or thematically with the preceding text(s), featuring two of the following question types (as in Proficiency Paper 3, Section A):
- blank-filling (using authentic texts)
- sentence transformation
- sentence completion

Oral and Written Practice

Communication tasks of the following types, based on ideas explored in the unit theme:

– Picture discussion (as in Proficiency Interview, Paper 5)
– Discussion topic or communication activity (as in Proficiency Interview, Paper 5)
– Composition-type exercises (as in Proficiency Composition, Paper 2)

Generally, no hard and fast guidelines are given for discussion topics and communication activities; the individual teacher will wish to adapt the material to class numbers, students' needs, course objectives, etc. Units 4, 5, 12, 17 and 19 contain information-gap activities for pair/group work. These can be found in the Communication Activities section on page 136. In Units 8 and 11, if it is decided to do the role-play activities, it is important that the students should be given enough time to prepare their roles. Some performances could be videoed; this would be especially useful for any later debriefing session(s).

Tests

After every two general topics, there is a multiple-choice vocabulary test (as in Proficiency Paper 1, Section A). All the vocabulary tested appears in the immediately preceding five units. Committing to memory and then reactivating new vocabulary always presents a potential problem for students, and the tests will help to reinforce new vocabulary items.

Answer Key

Answers to all exercises (where necessary) are given in the Answer Key at the back of the book. It should be pointed out that for some of the Use of English questions, the answers are by no means exhaustive. It is quite possible that teachers or students will come up with alternative, equally valid answers. For the context questions there are various ways of expressing the required information, and the answers given are merely suggestions. The last question is always a summary of the whole, or a part, of the passage and in the Proficiency examination an impression mark is given for such things as relevance, conciseness, fluency, avoidance of 'lifting' (attempts to paraphrase are appreciated), punctuation, spelling and general sentence structure. Examination candidates should be made aware of this.

Author's Acknowledgements

I would like to thank my colleagues at the Canterbury School of English, Geneva, for trialling the material. I am especially grateful to Mike Crowe, whose helpful comments and suggestions did so much to shape the final version.

Thanks must also go to Tony Hancock in West Germany, Tom Dodd in Italy and Tony Deamer in Japan for trialling and reporting on some of the material.

And, finally, special thanks to Simone, my wife, for her help and support, in particular for some immaculate typing under intense pressure.

Phil Bowman, Geneva, 1988.

Unit 1

Monarchy — are we being brainwashed?

Reading comprehension

You will find after each of the following passages a number of statements, each with four suggested endings. Choose the answer which you think fits best.

First passage

QUEEN OF HEARTS

After her jubilee service in 1977, she began, as monarchs before her had not done, to walk about among the crowds. Women split their faces into huge,
5 infatuated smiles; children waved little flags; men turned pink with pleasure, and one unfortunate failed to see her at all as he took a photograph of her instead. These people wanted her, liked
10 her, valued her. The reign was not a failure.

Now she is sixty; she has been ruling for thirty-four years. We will have the celebrations and the pictures again and
15 she will look—well, radiant. What else do you say about the Queen? And once again we wonder what on earth it is that makes a queen a success, and what place a sovereign has at all in a supposedly
20 logical society.

Elizabeth II's grasp on the national subconscious might well seem in line with a mother-goddess role—an asto-
25 nishing sixty-five per cent of us apparently dream about her. Certainly, the idea of an anointed monarch is quite irrational enough to get mixed up with religion. The Queen herself took her
30 coronation to be a deeply religious experience, and had the Duchess of Norfolk do her rehearsing for her up and down, over and over again, because it would have been sacrilegious to go through the motions herself.
35 What do people see in the Queen? Many people think of her as a being from another world, but then are quite overcome when she turns out to be human after all. Anyone who says any-
40 thing disparaging about royals gets hate letters of a violence—and sometimes of a disgustingness—that makes one wonder if the senders are quite sane.

It is a measure of the Queen's success
45 that she has seemed to embody what the most ordinary among her subjects want—and one of the things they want is a certain amount of dignity, mystery even.

(From the *Observer Review*)

1 It seems that the Queen
   A is infatuated with her subjects.
   B is generally popular.
   C has been a total success.
   D loves meeting ordinary people.

2 The writer
   A doesn't know why the Queen is a success.
   B attributes her success to the length of her reign.
   C believes that her success is logical.
   D doesn't know if she is a success.

3 The writer
   A says the Queen acts the part of a holy, maternal figure.
   B says the Queen is regarded by her subjects as a holy, maternal figure.
   C compares the Queen to a holy, maternal figure.
   D says the Duchess of Norfolk regards the Queen as a holy, maternal figure.

4 The Queen refused to rehearse for her coronation herself because
   A the Duchess of Norfolk would do it better than her.
   B she wanted to watch someone else go through the motions.
   C she believed it would be an irreverent act.
   D she wanted to save herself for the actual ceremony.

5 Many people
   A think it is inappropriate that the Queen should be human.
   B believe the Queen is an extra-terrestrial.
   C are confused or embarrassed when the Queen displays human qualities.
   D believe that the Queen is inhuman.

6 According to the passage, people who criticise the Queen
   A receive disgusting letters.
   B receive unpleasant letters.
   C are hated by the Royal Family.
   D are unpopular with the rest of her subjects.

Second passage

Monarchical sentiment is learnt, like any other social custom. It is taught as
we are taught to speak English and to say 'please' and 'thank you'.
   The process of indoctrination starts early. History in our schools is still
often taught by reference to reigns of kings and queens. Royal photographs
5 appear daily in newspapers, in women's magazines and on television. There
are, endlessly, parades of toy soldiers on beautiful horses—horses which live
better than old-age pensioners. We have our national slogans: 'For King and
Country', when soldiers are needed for savage wars; toasts 'To the Queen' at
every business dinner or Tory nosh-up. We talk about 'The King's (or the
10 Queen's) English'—which is only another dialect. Big rugby and football
matches are preceded by brass bands playing the National Anthem—to the
great irritation of fans on the terraces and players on the field. But they still
conform. It's the done thing—and who the hell cares, anyway? Not so long
ago, every cinema in the country had to play the National Anthem at the end
15 of each day's programmes. The rush to get out of the doors before 'The

Queen' came upon the screen grew too embarrassing and the rule was relaxed. And, every Sunday, those who attend an established church service must pray for the whole of the Royal Family. The House of Commons does it every day. Less than a dozen MPs attend.

(From *My Queen and I* by W. Hamilton)

7   The writer suggests that
   A   everyone in Britain has been brainwashed into supporting the Royal Family.
   B   The Royal Family's popularity is due to what is taught at school.
   C   monarchy cannot last.
   D   reverence for the Royal Family is the result of a form of brainwashing.

8   Royal publicity
   A   indoctrinates everyone.
   B   can be found anywhere.
   C   is part of people's daily lives.
   D   is harmful.

9   The rule about playing the National Anthem in cinemas was relaxed because
   A   most people couldn't be bothered to wait for it.
   B   most people were embarrassed by it.
   C   the cinema managers were embarrassed by it.
   D   most people were in a rush to get home.

10   According to the text, most MPs
   A   feel that praying for the Royal Family is wrong.
   B   seem to feel the same indifference towards Royal protocol as cinema goers used to.
   C   are irreligious.
   D   do not attend an established church service.

Use of English

A   Fill each of the numbered blanks in the following passage with **one** suitable word.

The Monarchy in Liechtenstein

I was struck by the universal and unquestioning loyalty .... (1) the Princely house—an unusual .... (2) in the last third of the twentieth .... (3). But it is .... (4). I talked to a number of people about it and their combined, unanimous view .... (5) like this: 'We are snobs—like everyone .... (6), all .... (7) the world. We prefer to have a .... (8) Habsburg prince rather .... (9) some obscure president. Secondly, the Prince is a nice, likeable .... (10) and his wife is .... (11) much loved. .... (12), the Prince is .... (13) only much better than a .... (14) would be, ... (15) is also much cheaper. He .... (16) us nothing. When he needs .... (17) he sells a Leonardo or .... (18), and he is .... (19) funds for years to ....(20).'

B Finish each of the following sentences in such a way that it means the same as the sentence printed before it.

    EXAMPLE: That table is so heavy that he can't lift it.
               That table is too ....
    ANSWER: *That table is too heavy for him to lift.*

1 She walked about among the crowds, as monarchs before her had not done.
  It was the first ....

2 She has been ruling for thirty-four years.
  It is ....

3 The Queen took her coronation to be a deeply religious experience.
  As far as the Queen ....

4 She had the Duchess of Norfolk do her rehearsing for her.
  The Duchess of Norfolk was ....

5 Anyone who says anything disparaging about royals gets hate letters.
  Hate letters ....

6 The process of indoctrination starts early.
  Indoctrination ....

7 The royal horses live better than old-age pensioners.
  Old-age pensioners lead ....

8 Big rugby and football matches are preceded by brass bands playing the National Anthem.
  Before ....

9 As soon as the film ended, everyone rushed to the exit.
  No sooner ....

10 Less than a dozen MPs attend.
  The number ....

Oral and written practice

Picture discussion
Look at the picture below and then answer the questions which follow.

1 Try to describe the picture literally.
2 What idea do you think this picture symbolises?
3 Could you suggest an appropriate title for this picture?
4 Does your country have a monarchy?
5 Do you think that a monarchy has any useful function these days?

Discussion topic
1 Some years ago, a national newspaper in Britain conducted a survey on attitudes to the Royal Family. The results indicated that more than sixty per cent of those people interviewed believed that the monarchy was divinely established. Do you find this surprising? Explain why/why not. If the same survey were carried out today, do you think the results would be different?

2   QUEEN STRUCK BY ANTI-MONARCHY PLACARD
   Imagine that the above phrase is a newspaper headline. You will be given a few minutes to think of **your** version of the accompanying story before you tell it to the other members of your group. You may make a few brief notes to help you remember the story you are going to tell. Listen to and comment on other people's versions of the story and ask them questions too, if you wish.

Written work
1 Look at the following statements, all of which have been made about monarchy. Choose three, and comment on each in a paragraph of not more than 100 words.

a *The Royal Family presents the British people with a kind of continuous soap opera at the centre of their national life.*

b *Royals everywhere, particularly the British Royal Family, are under constant pressure from the media, who continually harass them and don't allow them a moment's relaxation.*

c *The Royal Family do an incredible job. They're the greatest tourist attraction that any country has ever had.*

d *The institution of monarchy is an instrument used to make respectable to the unthinking and the irrational a social and economic class system which is unfair, divisive and often cruel.*

e *The British Royal Family is one of the richest families in the world and should be made to account for every penny of its vast private wealth before any more public money is squandered on them. Their total wealth, of course, remains a closely guarded secret, for they have always refused to reveal the actual figures.*

f *The notion of hereditary monarchy is as foolish as it is infamous. What is this office which idiots and infants are capable of filling? Some talent is required to be a common workman; to be a king or queen no more is needed than to have a human form.*

2 Write a composition (about 350 words) on the following topic: 'Has hereditary monarchy any place in a modern democracy?'

Unit 2

Democracy or a Class System?

Reading comprehension

Read the following passage, and then answer the questions which follow it.

Although every society recognizes the need for some kind of leadership, democracy tries to make its leaders as little authoritarian as possible, and by giving each man a vote, and therefore at least a nominal share in the election of government, has attempted to diminish the gap between those who govern and
5 those who are governed. The revolutionary ideology of liberty, equality and fraternity is essentially opposed to an authoritarian, hierarchical structure of society; and innate differences of strength, or even intelligence, between individuals are only grudgingly recognized. Aristocratic societies have a firmly established rank order, originally based upon dominance, though later super-
10 seded by inheritance. In such societies, each man knows his place; and the more he is content to regard his lot as ordained by fate, the more stable is the structure of the whole. The aggressive potential of the group is disposed hierarchically in such a way that each man dominates the next below him in rank until the lowliest peasant is reached—and it may be assumed that his aggression is fully engaged in
15 wresting a meagre existence from the land which he is compelled to cultivate. Modern democracies have moved some way from this more primitive pattern, though not so far as most liberal-minded persons would like to think. In doing so, they have set themselves a problem in the disposal of aggression. The way in which they have solved this is to allow an opposition—a feature of democracy not
20 tolerated by authoritarian societies. If men are to join together in an egalitarian way as a band of brothers rather than exercising power over one another in a descending scale, they need an opposition, another band holding opposing opinions, against whom they can cooperatively strive. Needless to say, no human society is completely consistent with either the authoritarian or the democratic
25 pattern, but the trend is not difficult to determine, and the consequences which follow are important.

It has long been realized amongst men, as amongst baboons, that if group cohesion is the main objective, democratic principles must go by the board. Even democracies support armies; and military organization is based upon a strict rank
30 order and absolute obedience. The dress of soldiers is misnamed 'uniform'; for, although an officer may garb himself in the same colour as a private, his rank will

be emphasized by tabs or badges which indicate that he is far from being uniform in status. The whole of military training is designed to inculcate the notion that men are by no means equal. From the commander-in-chief down to the lowliest private, each man knows his place and must obey his superior without question; and whilst any show of aggression towards authority is severely discouraged, there is a good deal of opportunity for aggressive display towards inferiors, as any man who has experienced the verbal onslaught of a sergeant-major will surely agree. Frederick II of Prussia is said to have insisted that a soldier must fear his officer more than the enemy. As in the case of baboons, this hierarchical structure makes for stability; so that the large aggregations of human beings which make up an army act together as one. It is hardly possible to imagine that the coherence of so extensive a group could be maintained in any other way.

(From *Human Aggression* by Anthony Storr)

1 According to the writer, what quality in a leader would be most unwelcome in a democracy?
2 Why are differences of strength and intelligence only 'grudgingly recognized' (line 8)?
3 What is the structure of an aristocratic society based on nowadays?
4 Explain the phrase 'he is content to regard his lot as ordained by fate' (line 11).
5 'He' (line 15) refers to . . .?
6 'They' (line 18) refers to . . .?
7 'This' (line 19) refers to . . .?
8 What is 'the trend' referred to in line 25?
9 What is meant by the phrase 'go by the board' (line 28)?
10 Explain the writer's use of 'even' (line 28).
11 Why is 'uniform' an inappropriate word for soldiers' clothing?
12 What would 'the verbal onslaught of a sergeant-major' (line 38) be?
13 Why should Frederick II of Prussia have insisted that a soldier must be more frightened of his superior than the enemy?
14 What does the writer suggest would be the result if armies ceased to be based on a hierarchical system?
15 Summarise, in a paragraph of not more than 120 words, the ways in which military organisation differs from the basic structure of a democratic system.

Use of English

A Fill each of the numbered blanks in the following passage with **one** suitable word.

The idea that the twentieth century is the age of the common man has .... (1) one of the great clichés of .... (2) time. The same old .... (3) are put .... (4) in evidence: monarchy .... (5) a system of government has been .... (6) discredited; the monarchies that survive have been deprived of .... (7) political power; inherited wealth has been savagely reduced .... (8) taxation and, ... (9) time, the great fortunes will .... (10) altogether. In a number of countries the victory has been complete. The people rule; the great millenium has become a political reality. But has it? .... (11) examination doesn't bear .... (12) the claim. It is a fallacy to suppose that all men are .... (13) and that society will be levelled out if you provide everybody with the .... (14) educational opportunities. The fact is that nature dispenses brains and ability .... (15) total disregard for the principal of equality. The spread of education has destroyed the old class .... (16) and created a new one. Rewards are based .... (17) merit. For 'aristocracy' read 'meritocracy'; .... (18) other respects, society .... (19) unchanged: the class system is rigidly .... (20).

B For each of the sentences below, write a new sentence as similar as possible in meaning to the original sentence, but using the word given in **bold** letters. This word **must not be altered** in any way.

    EXAMPLE: It wasn't my intention to frighten you.
                mean
    ANSWER: *I didn't mean to frighten you.*

1 Although every society recognises the need for leadership, democracy tries to have unauthoritarian leaders.
   despite
   ....

2 Dominance was later superseded by inheritance.
   place
   ....

3 The trend is not difficult to determine.
   can
   ....

4 The dress of soldiers is misnamed 'uniform'.
   inappropriate
   ....

5 Frederick II is said to have insisted that a soldier must fear his officer more than the enemy.
   it
   ....

6 This hierarchical structure makes for stability.
   stable
   ....

7 The monarchies that survive have been deprived of all political power.
   taken
   ....

8 The great millenium has become a political reality.
   turned
   ....

9 It's a fallacy to suppose all men are equal.
   supposition
   ....

10 The spread of education has destroyed the old class system and created a new one.
    replaced
    ....

Oral and written practice

Picture discussion
Look at the two pictures below and answer the questions which follow.

1 Describe the people in the pictures.
2 Does anything strike you as unusual in the left-hand picture?
3 Bearing in mind what was said about the left-hand picture in question 2, what conclusion would you draw about the magazine in the right-hand picture?
4 Are you personally aware of class differences and do you feel you belong to a particular class?
5 Is there a hierarchical system in operation in your country? If so, is it based on social status, money or on something else?

Discussion topic
Do you agree with any of the following statements?

People are born unequal, therefore it's normal that the structure of society should reflect these inequalities.

The problem with a democracy is that the working classes are allowed to vote. In my opinion they are clearly unfit to vote.

Just as women enjoy being dominated by men, so the lower classes enjoy being dominated by their social betters.

Written work
1 Write a short story (about 350 words), ending with the sentence: 'I never realised he/she was such a snob.'
2 Write a composition (about 350 words) on the following topic: 'An equal society is an impossible dream.'

Unit 3

A Sloane Ranger Speaks

Reading comprehension

The following text has been broken up into five parts, which have then been mixed up. Decide what the correct sequence should be.

a

The right clothes are essential to the Sloanes' courting ritual. It helps them to recognise each other. Katie said proudly: "The Sloane mode of dress isn't glamorous. It's elegant and down-to-earth. We're the more homely type. I couldn't bear being the ultra-glam woman who has to look a million dollars 24 hours a day. I just wouldn't be able to do it. A Sloane's life is too busy to be glamorous. We always have to arrange for someone to look after the house, take the dogs for walks and see to the horses. You couldn't possibly go tottering around on stilettos in a fur coat in the middle of the country.

"Sloanes are sexy in a low-key sort of way. They most certainly don't flaunt it. I love what we wear and how we hold ourselves. But a Sloane man is much more likely than an ordinary man to turn round when he passes a pretty Sloane girl. We respond to each other. We wear our clothes with confidence and breeding and you can't beat that.

"Clothes are investments to us. I will pay hundreds of pounds for garments that will last for years and won't go out of style. I have my ballgowns made by a dressmaker, or I hire them, because all the same people see you at the balls and you'd have to spend a fortune to buy a different dress every time. Sloanes are actually very thrifty. We spend a lot on clothes and jewellery but always save on food. We'll make do with watered-down scrambled eggs and baked beans."

Sex, which these extraordinary people call banging, is a taboo subject, and presumably only takes place when every other jolly pastime has been exhausted. Katie coughed into her ruffled collar: "You simply don't talk about sex. That would be vulgar. You let everybody get on with their own lives but never dig into it, although Sloanes are very broadminded.

"A Sloane's idea of ultimate fun is spraying champagne at people, doing silly things like throwing food around the room and skinny-dipping in Hyde Park. We have such good fun that we don't think we look ridiculous. Life is worth living and one must have a cracking good time if one's a Sloane. If we have any worries we don't think about them. We don't let them spoil our fun. You'll never find a moping Sloane."

b

There is a rare, protected species lurking among the ordinary British people. They are born with a whole collection of silver spoons in their mouths, which might account for the high-pitched, plummy way they speak.

Their natural habitat is London's elegant Knightsbridge, usually within a stone's throw of Sloane Square. But at weekends they flock towards England's finer country houses and there their feet instantly turn green—encased in wellies of the hunting, shooting and fishing variety, even if they're only walking the dog. When in town, the foliage of the female changes dramatically to good, solid navy-blue. This sensible outfit must be boosted by a string of pearls, ruffled collar, and flat shoes like Princess Di used to wear. The male is recognisable by his heavy shoes, cord or tweed trousers, lumberjack-type shirt and cravat. He will, of course, have a spotted silk handkerchief in the top pocket of his herringbone jacket.

They are the Sloanes, a wealthy pack of privileged, fun-loving folk who don't just think they're above the ordinary masses, they're utterly convinced of it. The Hooray Henrys and Henriettas of Sloaneland hate to be infected by close contact with lesser species, but love rubbing shoulders with each other.

A typical member of the Sloane tribe, 20-year-old Katie Harvey, trilled: "Every morning I just about manage the absolutely frightful Tube journey to work, pressed up against all the common people. Of course, if I was pressed up against a Barbour jacket on a Hooray Henry it would be quite superb, but a dirty old anorak is a different thing altogether." She is not the slightest bit concerned that people in anoraks—dirty or not— might be similarly unimpressed at the thought of rumbling along the District Line staring up at the nostrils of someone with her nose neatly pointed towards the sky.

Katie's background and breeding gives her an impeccable Sloane pedigree. She hails from a wealthy Staffordshire family, and was looked after by a string of French au pairs in their large farmhouse, crammed with antiques and paintings. She said: "My privileged home-life filled me with confidence and pride, and I learned to assert myself at boarding-school."

Now that Katie has left home to join up with her fellow nobles in Knightsbridge, the hunt for the right man has begun. Of course, she would never jeopardise her future comfort by falling in love with a working-class man. Katie smiled gracefully: "When a Sloane meets a new man, she finds out about the money situation straightaway. My circle of friends is full of extremely suitable partners, men who come from a similar background, have been away at school and are, naturally, very well-off."

c

8am: Katie crawls out of bed with a terrible hangover after the night's revels, and staggers across her ballgown to the kitchen for a strong cup of coffee. With her navy-blue suit and scarf in place, she arrives at the Tube platform just in time to meet all her fellow Sloanes. She said: "We catch up on any gossip and go over what everyone did the night before. It fortifies us to brave the smelly tube journey to work."

9am: At Harpers, with another cup of coffee, the more serious gossip of the day is launched. "We're mostly Sloanes there and we settle down to a jolly good chat. While I go through the post, I ring up all my other friends across London to catch up on the gossip. It's a very jolly, social time with all the girls together exchanging notes."

12.30pm: The next phase in gossip is carried out at a smart table in Fenwick, slightly early for lunch to ensure that there is no rubbing shoulders with the masses. "We laugh and giggle, we're loud and always noticed. My voice carries, as they say. After lunch, it's a question of buzzing through some work so that one can get away by 5.30 in time to start preparing for the evening's events. I couldn't possibly put up with the kind of job which could interfere in any way with my social life."

5.30pm: Katie stops by at Marks & Spencer to buy the food for that night's dinner party—usually melon, trout, a good honest pud and lots and lots of booze. "Sloane men love their stodge, so you've got to cater for that and, after three or four double gins and tonics each, we get stuck into a case of good wine. There's always lots of shouting and laughing, spraying champagne and throwing food at each other. After the coffee there must be port, always passed around to the left, and often some whisky too."

1am: Packed into a taxi, the noisy Sloane mob make their way to Ormonds disco to throw each other around the floor. Katie said: "Most nights I stagger home around three or four and the next day the cycle starts again.

"At weekends, I go to the country for a breath of fresh air, some sleep and a good walk with the dogs or horse riding. I use that time to recover so that I'm fighting fit for the parties the following week. Of course, all winter holidays are spent skiing and summers are passed at a choice of villas owned by friends in the South of France.

"It's a good life. I wouldn't change it for all the tea in China."

---

d

"If I fell madly in love with a dustman, I'd have to take a serious pause before deciding to marry him, because I'm sure that, within a few years, it would disintegrate due to class difference and lack of capital. My parents certainly wouldn't like it. They hope I'll go for the right man, and I will. The men I mix with are merchant bankers, chartered surveyors, stockbrokers, and those men at Cirencester Agricultural College. My search for the right chap takes me to a stream of drinks parties and dinners, and, of course, I go to balls all over the country and attend Royal Ascot and Henley Regatta. It's terribly important to be seen in all the right places at the right time and with all the right people. It doesn't matter at all if one is not remotely interested in horse racing or rowing."

Katie has already got a possible catch on the hook, and he's not a dustman. She screeched: "He's the right sort, all right. He's at Cirencester Agricultural College, lives on a farm and comes from excellent stock. Naturally he shoots, rides and skis. If we got married, I'd like to have three children, two boys and a girl, who I'd name James, Charles and Lucy, and then I could play around with lots of middle names. We would live in the country and have a town house in London for shopping purposes. Naturally, I'd inherit the good family silver, furniture and any jewellery worth handing down.

"One of the most important things in a successful Sloane marriage is organisational ability. The lady must be able to arrange the right home-help. If you find a good woman who can darn the socks as well as keep the house in order, you've got it made, and I hope I could organise that. It would be quite unthinkable for a person such as myself to waste her time doing the sort of menial chores that you can so easily get an ordinary person to do for you."

The Queen of the Sloanes, Princess Di, caught the best man of all. Quite brill really. Katie said: "Prince Charles is the ultimate Sloane man. He's so sweet and lovely. He's obviously not the dashing, debonair hunk that Prince Andrew is, but there's clearly a lot to him and he tries really hard. I think he's wonderful. Prince Andrew is terribly good-looking, so obviously throughout his life he's had women falling at his feet, and he's headed for the glam, sexy sort. However, I always doubted he'd marry one. I just felt that he'd settle down and return to his own kind in the end.

"Princess Di is the SuperSloane and we all try and copy her as much as possible. It's incredible the way she's changed from Prince Charles' blushing fiancée into an amazingly beautiful, confident Princess. I went to a ball she was at and she's got a wonderful aura and magnetism around her. You feel her presence above anyone else's. It helps that she's able to wear fabulous clothes, but she certainly knows how to carry them off. She's got ultimate style. She wears lots of classic outfits—and so do most Sloanes—clothes that don't date and are then jazzed up with lots of jewellery and scarves."

e

Even when they're running riot, Sloanes are particular about the music they'll dance to. Katie scoffed: "We only like the right pop stars, certainly not the heavy metal types. Elton John's acceptable and Phil Collins is great because he went to boarding-school. Duran Duran and Wham have such a following of screaming 12-year-olds that one wouldn't want to be around them, and, of course, they don't seem to be able to string a sentence together. They come out with ridiculous statements. I think of Boy George with raised eyebrows. He's not quite the thing, is he? Madonna's rather vulgar, but I do like Annie Lennox. Anyone who can have her hair that short and still look stunning must be a decent sort."

The only thing Sloanes really rate higher than themselves is Queen and country. Katie said: "I'm very, very patriotic and the epitome of that is the Royal Wedding and Silver Jubilee. All my deepest emotions came out then. I admire the Queen tremendously because she's so confident. You can just tell she's very much the boss and she's also very feminine. It's lovely the way people respect her and you know she'd never put up with any nonsense. She has a terrific hold over her family without keeping them on a ball and chain. I'd go a long way for my Queen, and the ultimate Sloane achievement for me would be to become a Royal lady-in-waiting. It would be the sort of position I've been trained for. Not the kind of thing for ordinary people."

Sloanes are oblivious to the sneers of the rest of the country.

Katie wailed: "I'm proud to be a Sloane Ranger, but when I walk down the street, people shout out 'Snob' at me because I'm wearing smart clothes and have a certain bearing. They shout, "There goes a Sloane,' but I always keep a dignified silence. What's wrong with us after all? Sloanes have always been around and we will go on being there."

Katie is sharing a two-bedroomed flat in Kensington with just the right sort of girl, Tania Fforbes-Parkinson-Smyth and, of course, it's owned by Tania's parents. It's extremely un-Sloane to be too enthusiastic about a career, but fortunately Katie works at Harpers And Queen glossy magazine, the highest form of Sloane literature.

A typical day in her absolutely topping life might go something like this . . .

(From the *News of the World Sunday Magazine*)

Vocabulary
Find words or phrases in the text which correspond to the following definitions.

a
1 practical
2 extremely attractive; sexy
3 walking unsteadily
4 restrained; understated; not exaggerated.

5 show off; try to attract attention to
 6 economical; careful about spending money
 7 something which is a forbidden topic of conversation
 8 enquire about; show excessive curiosity about
 9 nude bathing/swimming
10 depressed; in low spirits

b
 1 hiding; existing without being obvious
 2 born into a rich or influential family
 3 within a short distance of
 4 travel in great numbers
 5 meeting and mixing with
 6 inferior classes of people
 7 spoke/said in a high-pitched musical way
 8 in close physical proximity to/contact with
 9 empty-headed, young upper-class male
10 endanger; put in danger

c
 1 unpleasant feeling after drinking too much alcohol
 2 noisy festivities/celebrations
 3 walks unsteadily
 4 talk (often malicious) about other people
 5 gives strength to
 6 laugh in a nervous or silly way
 7 doing quickly and casually
 8 alcohol
 9 heavy, solid food
10 in excellent physical condition

d
 1 break up
 2 money (that can be used to produce more money)
 3 future husband
 4 passing from one person to another by inheritance
 5 mend (something knitted)
 6 work suitable for a servant
 7 fantastic; super
 8 physically attractive male
 9 manage to do something difficult with ease and assurance
10 given more life; made superficially more attractive

e
 1 behaving in a noisy, undisciplined way
 2 mocked; spoke contemptuously
 3 construct
 4 say; utter
 5 marvellous; wonderful
 6 embodiment; small-scale example
 7 tolerate
 8 totally unaware of
 9 contemptuous remarks
10 way of standing/walking/behaving

Use of English

A   Finish each of the following sentences in such a way that it means the same as the sentence printed before it.

   EXAMPLE: That table is so heavy that he can't lift it.
            That table is too ....
   ANSWER: *That table is too heavy for him to lift.*

1   Their natural habitat is London's elegant Knightsbridge.
    They normally ....

2   If I was pressed up against a Hooray Henry, it would be quite superb.
    Were ....

3   Katie's background and breeding gives her an impeccable Sloane pedigree.
    Because of her ....

4   She would never jeopardise her future comfort by falling in love with a working-class man.
    At no time ....

5   Throughout his life he's had women falling at his feet.
    Women ....

6   She's got a wonderful aura and magnetism about her.
    A wonderful ....

7   A Sloane's life is too busy to be glamorous.
    A Sloane's life is so ....

8   A Sloane man is much more likely than an ordinary man to turn around.
    An ordinary man ....

9   We'll make do with watered-down scrambled eggs and baked beans.
    Watered-down scrambled eggs ....

10 A Sloane's idea of ultimate fun is spraying champagne at people.
    Ultimate fun ....

B   Fill each of the blanks in the following passage with a suitable phrase.

   EXAMPLE: .... tennis in that heat, you would have been exhausted.
   ANSWER: *If you had played . . .*

A Conversation in a Country Pub

'What about that judge .... (1)
that miner a year for poaching the other week? Did you read about that, Jack?'

'Read about it. I should think so. Those days are over though now, everybody keeps telling me.'
'It served him right. .... first
time he'd been done. Some folk never learn.'

'I know, but bloody hell. A year for a few brace of pheasant. It's a bit stiff, isn't it?'

'He .... (3) trespassing. He
knew what to expect.'

'Trespassing. And where ....
land from in the first place, anyway? They just grabbed it, didn't they? Or the king

dished it out to courtiers and pimps and royal bastards born on the wrong side of the blanket. That's .... (5) it from, so don't talk to me about trespassing, George.'

Frank started to laugh.

'It's like that joke Soft Mick once told us, about when the old Duke met that miner up on the moor. He said the old Duke was out walking on one of his moors, ... (6) this miner with his gun under his arm. Anyway, they had a big argument about private property and trespassing and suchlike, and in the end the Duke finished up saying, "Do you know my ancestors had to fight for this land, my man?" And the miner said, "Right then, get your coat off and .... (7) for it now." '

Jack was not amused.

'He was a bastard, the old Duke. He was as hard as nails with poachers, especially the miners who worked at his pits. Straight to court, no messing, then it was a heavy fine or prison. .... (8) best to discourage them. He had to, because when they'd had a good night's poaching, they .... (9) work for the rest of the week.'

The gamekeeper turned round from the bar.

'The law's the law, Jack. And that's all there is to it.'

'Yes, but whose law is it, George? That's what I want to know. The Duke and the judges and suchlike, ... (10) same team, aren't they? Everybody knows that.'

Oral and written practice

Picture discussion
Look at the photograph below and then answer the questions which follow.

1 Who do you suppose these people are?
2 Describe what is happening in the photograph.
3 Why do you think these people are behaving in this way?
4 Can you think of a situation where you might be tempted to behave like this?
5 Have you ever seen people behave like this in public? If so, describe the event.

Discussion topic

Which of the following adjectives, in your opinion, would accurately describe Katie?

frivolous, profound, empty-headed, intellectual, industrious, idle, ambitious, privileged, arrogant, humble, snobbish, abstemious, self-indulgent, extrovert, introvert, calculating, impetuous, selfish, altruistic, tolerant.

Support your opinions with evidence from the text if possible.

Can you think of any other adjectives that would apply to Katie?

Written work

1 The following quotes have been taken from the text at the beginning of the unit. Choose four and comment on them in four paragraphs of about 50 words each.

a *Every morning I just about manage the absolutely frightful Tube journey to work, pressed up against all the common people.*

b *When a Sloane meets a new man, she finds out about the money situation straightaway.*

c *It would be quite unthinkable for a person such as myself to waste her time doing the sort of menial chores that you can so easily get an ordinary person to do for you.*

d *A Sloane's life is too busy to be glamorous.*

e *We spend a lot on clothes and jewellery but always save on food.*

f *A Sloane's idea of ultimate fun is spraying champagne at people and throwing food around the room.*

g *I'm very patriotic and the epitome of that is the Royal Wedding and Silver Jubilee. All my deepest emotions came out then. I admire the Queen tremendously because she's so confident. It's lovely the way people respect her.*

h *The ultimate Sloane achievement for me would be to become a Royal lady-in-waiting. It would be the sort of position I've been trained for. Not the kind of thing for ordinary people.*

2 Write a composition (about 350 words) on the following topic: 'Inheriting money and property is wrong.' Discuss.

Unit 4

The Rich Kids

Reading comprehension

Read the following passage, and then decide whether the statements which follow it are true or false. Be prepared to justify your answers. If you feel that there is not enough evidence to justify true or false, put a question mark.

Life really should be one long journey of joy for children born with a world of wealth at their tiny feet. But psychologists now believe that silver spoons can
5 leave a bitter taste. If suicide statistics are an indicator of happiness, then the rich are a miserable lot. Figures show that it is the wealthy who most often do away with themselves.
10 Internationally famous child psychiatrist Dr. Robert Coles is the world's top expert on the influence of money on children. He has written a highly-acclaimed book on the subject,
15 *The Privileged Ones*, and his research shows that too much money in the family can cause as many problems as too little. "Obviously there are certain advantages to being rich," says the
20 53-year-old psychiatrist, "such as better health, education and future work prospects. But most important is the quality of family life. Money can't buy love."

It can buy a lot of other things,
25 though, and that's where the trouble starts. Rich kids have so much to choose from that they often become confused. Over-indulgence by their parents can make them spoilt. They tend to travel
30 more than other children, from home to home and country to country, which causes feelings of restlessness.

"But privileged children do have a better sense of their positions in the
35 world," adds Mr Coles, "and they are more self-assured. I can't imagine, for instance, that Prince William will not grow up to be self-assured." Prince William is probably the most privileged
40 child in the world and will grow up to fill the world's most privileged position— King of England. It is a fact that no-one knows how much the Queen is worth. There are the royal estates—two
45 palaces, two castles and a country mansion. There's also the royal picture collection, the stamp collection, the library, the jewels and the royal yacht Britannia. Before he inherits that lot,
50 William will succeed his father as Prince of Wales and enjoy the income from the Duchy of Cornwall, currently worth 771,480 pounds a year. Known jokingly around the Palace as West Country
55 Limited, the Duchy consists of 26,600 acres of Cornwall including mineral rights for tin mining and 2,000 acres of forestry. It also owns the Oval cricket

ground, 900 flats in London, oyster beds
60 and a golf course.

So money will never be one of Prince William's problems. Living anything that resembles a normal life will. "He will have a sense of isolation," cautions
65 Dr. Coles, "and he could suffer from the handicap of not being able to deal with the everyday world because he will never really be given the chance. Royals

exist in an elaborate social fantasy.
70 Everything they have achieved is because of an accident of birth. There can be no tremendous inner satisfaction about that."

Today's wealthy parents perhaps real-
75 ise their riches can be more of a burden than a blessing to their children. So their priority is to ensure that their families are as rich in love as they are in money.

(From the *Sunday Mirror*)

1 Rich children are embittered.
2 There is a higher incidence of suicide amongst the rich than amongst the poor.
3 Some people have criticised Dr Robert Coles' book.
4 Coles believes that there are as many advantages to being poor as there are to being rich.
5 Rich children can be deprived of the thing they are most in need of.
6 Rich children are rarely given too many material things.
7 Rich children don't get enough rest.
8 It is unlikely that Prince William will have a great deal of self-confidence.
9 The Queen doesn't know how much money she has.
10 Prince William's income from the Duchy of Cornwall will be worth over three-quarters of a million pounds.
11 West Country Limited is a nickname.
12 Prince William will have no idea of how normal people lead their lives.
13 Prince William will probably not be required to adapt to the normal world.
14 Coles suggests that members of the Royal Family have not earned what they have.
15 Most wealthy parents are aware of the problems that their money can bring.

Vocabulary

A   Find words or phrases in the passage which correspond to the following definitions.

1 kill
2 praised by many people
3 expectations
4 satisfying someone's desires to an excessive degree
5 very large, impressive house
6 money received
7 at the present time
8 feel lonely
9 handle
10 complex

B Explain the meaning of the following words and phrases taken from the passage.

1. silver spoons can leave a bitter taste (ll 4–5)
2. restlessness (l 32)
3. that lot (l 49)
4. succeed (l 50)
5. mineral rights (ll 56–57)
6. oyster beds (l 59)
7. social fantasy (l 69)
8. an accident of birth (l 71)
9. more of a burden than a blessing (ll 75–76)
10. priority (l 77)

Use of English

A   Fill each of the numbered blanks in the following passage with **one** suitable word.

Paul McCartney is Britain's top earner. He .... (1) a staggering £25 million a year. That's £68,493 a day! Or .... (2) than £47 a minute! .... (3) neither he, nor his family, maintain any of the outward trappings of .... (4) phenomenal wealth. .... (5) with Linda, his wife of fourteen years, her nineteen-year-old daughter, Heather, and their children, Mary, twelve, Stella, ten, and four-year-old James, he .... (6) lives in a two-bedroomed cottage in the Sussex countryside. They have a huge mansion in London's St. John's Wood, where they .... (7) to live until Paul decided he did not like the .... (8) 'privileged' kids his children were mixing .... (9). He talked to Linda about it. Together, they decided it was .... (10) to live an ordinary life. So these days there is no chauffeur, no housekeeper, no cook, no nanny. 'I .... (11) up in a house with a cook and a nanny and that has put me .... (12),' American-born Linda explained. 'When you have a nanny, your kids end .... (13) calling her "mummy". I didn't grow up as close .... (14) my mother as I would have liked.' The McCartneys .... (15) take their holidays in the Bahamas and fly by Concorde when they travel to America, but at home .... (16) is ever so humble. They could .... (17) caviare and champagne every day; instead, they prefer simpler fare. 'I .... (18) all the cooking, which is a bit like .... (19) a cafe,' said Linda. 'But then .... (20) do thousands of other mothers with large families.'

B   For each of the sentences below, write a new sentence as similar as possible in meaning to the original sentence, but using the word given in **bold** letters. This word **must not be altered** in any way.

EXAMPLE: It wasn't my intention to frighten you.
 mean
ANSWER: *I didn't mean to frighten you.*

1   It is the wealthy who most often do away with themselves.
 commit

     ....

2   Dr Robert Coles is the world's top expert on this subject.
    anyone
    ....

3   He has written a book, 'The Privileged Ones'.
    title
    ....

4   They have so much to choose from that they become confused.
    cause
    ....

5   Travelling around causes feelings of restlessness.
    makes
    ....

6   I can't imagine that Prince William will not be self-assured.
    find
    ....

7   William will succeed his father as Prince of Wales.
    next
    ....

8   The Duchy consists of 26,000 acres of Cornwall.
    composed
    ....

9   He will have a sense of isolation.
    isolated
    ....

10 They can feel no inner satisfaction about that.
    inwardly
    ....

Oral and written practice

Communication activity
You will be asked to look at a communication activity (1, 7 or 13) at the back of
the book. You will then be asked to take part in a conversation with a group of
other students or with your teacher.

Written work
1   Write a composition (about 350 words) on the following topic:
    'Money doesn't necessarily make you happy – but it certainly helps.'
2   Douglas Branson has been unemployed for some time and is deeply in
    debt. One morning a letter arrives, informing him that a long-lost relative
    in Australia has just died and left him a large amount of money. Write
    the report of this story (about 300 words) which appears in the local
    newspaper.

Picture discussion

Look at the photograph below and answer the questions which follow.

1 Would you say that these two children had been born with a silver spoon in their mouth? Why/why not?
2 Describe their physical appearance.
3 Do you think they look happy or sad? Explain why.
4 Where would you expect to see the sort of area shown in the photograph?
5 How do you think the lives of these two children differ from the lives of the children described in the passage at the beginning of this unit?

Unit 5

Value for Money?

Reading comprehension

You will find after the following passages a number of statements, each with four suggested endings. Choose the answer which you think fits best.

a

RENT-A-ROYAL CASH FURY

WELL - HEELED Americans are to pay £35,000 a couple to attend a ball with Prince Charles and Princess Diana.

Other guests will fork out £7,000 for a double ticket just to eat in the same room as the royal couple.

The rent-a-royal plan has infuriated locals in the ritzy Florida resort of Palm Beach.

Many are boycotting the charity ball, because they reckon Charles and Diana are being exploited.

The queen of the Palm Beach cocktail circuit, Mrs. Gregg Dodge, has already announced she will not attend the dinner-dance next week.

"That's the day I have my legs waxed," she said.

The £35,000 meal ticket includes a family snapshot with the Prince and Princess.

Society hostess Jan Terrana said: "I'm embarrassed for the royal couple.

"It's real exploitation, and I'm sure Charles and Diana have no idea this kind of thing is going on."

Eyebrows are also being raised at how invitations were sent out before the town council gave the go-ahead for a charity event. The prestigious ball is in aid of the United World Colleges Fund. Stars such as Joan Collins, Bob Hope, Cary Grant and Gregory Peck are expected to attend.

Its organisers hope to raise £1,400,000.

Palm Beach's British-born mayor Evelyn Marix said: "The amount of money being raised caused even more concern." Fund chairman Jack King said: "The money will provide scholarships for deserving students around the world to attend the United World colleges."

● Tory MP Dame Jill Knight slammed the American "hard sell" of Charles and Diana as "not appropriate or polite."

(From the *Sunday Mirror*)

b

£85,000 IN A DAY FOR JOAN!

A LIGHTNING visit to West Germany reaped Dynasty superstar Joan Collins a stagger-
5 ing £85,930—in just FIVE HOURS.

On Wednesday new-lywed Joan collected a thumping £20,000 for
10 presenting a jackpot cheque to Littlewoods pools winner George Newham in London.

It took 20 minutes—work-
15 ing out at £1,000 a minute, the same pay rate she earns as superbitch Alexis.

But her trip to Munich beat that.
20 First she made a ten-minute appearance on a chat show. FEE: £4,900.

Next she visited a famous furrier and gracefully
25 accepted a white mink cape. VALUE: £13,250.

Then a Munich jeweller presented her with a gold and emerald necklace.
30 VALUE: £7,700.

She picked up two white dream cars at a BMW show-room. VALUE: £55,280.
35 Last call was at the Hilton Hotel to draw a winning lottery ticket. FEE: £4,800.

(From the *News of the World*)

c

STORM OVER SELINA'S PAY

A ROW has erupted over sexy Selina Scott's new contract with the BBC's Break-
5 fast Time—believed to be at least £50,000 a year.

Furious Labour MP Tom
10 Torney urged Mrs Thatcher to reject the BBC's demands for a higher licence fee be-cause of this "preposterously inflated wage."
15 Mr Torney, MP for Brad-ford South, said: "How in the light of this absurd deci-sion can the BBC have the neck to ask for yet more money?
20 "Millions of poor and de-prived people will be shock-ed at this handout.

"They'll be forced, if the Government gives in, to pay
25 £65 a year for their licences, simply because the BBC overpays its prima donnas."

(From the *News of the World*)

Passage **a**

1 £35,000 entitled the guests to
  A attend the same banquet as the royal couple.
  B have their photograph taken and dance with the royal couple.
  C have their photograph taken with, eat with, and go to the same ball as the royal couple.
  D eat and have their legs waxed with the royal couple.

2 The infuriated locals believe
  A that the royal couple are unwitting pawns in the affair.
  B that the royal couple are overpriced and overprivileged.
  C that paying money to socialise with the royal couple is inappropriate.
  D that the organisers don't care if they embarrass the royal couple.

Passage **b**

3 On the two days in question, Joan Collins worked for
    A   an undisclosed amount of time.
    B   twenty minutes.
    C   thirty minutes.
    D   five hours.

4 In all, Joan Collins accepted
    A   three free gifts.
    B   four free gifts.
    C   a cheque and three free gifts.
    D   a lottery ticket and four free gifts.

Passage **c**

5 According to Tom Torney,
    A   Mrs Thatcher is against the BBC's demands for a higher licence fee.
    B   the higher licence fee would be unfair to the underprivileged members of society.
    C   the poor and unemployed are criticising the amount of Selina Scott's pay.
    D   the BBC overpays all its staff.

Vocabulary

A Find words or phrases in the passages which correspond to the following definitions.

Passage **a**
  1 rich
  2 pay (verb)
  3 made very angry; provoked to rage or fury
  4 luxurious and elegant
  5 refusing to have anything to do with/take part
  6 group of well-off people in a particular place who frequently socialise with each other
  7 people are expressing surprise
  8 criticised strongly

Passage **b**
  9 brought or earned (as a reward or payment)
 10 astonishing
 11 recently married
 12 enormous; huge
 13 extremely spiteful, malicious woman
 14 person who sells furs
 15 competition in which certain tickets chosen at random win prizes

Passage **c**
 16 broken out; begun
 17 considering; taking into account
 18 be cheeky enough to
 19 unearned amount of money
 20 stars or leading personalities (often spoilt and arrogant)

B Explain the meaning of the following words and phrases taken from the passages.

Passage **a**
1   resort (l 13)
2   charity ball (l 16)
3   exploited (ll 18–19)
4   snapshot (ll 29–30)
5   the go-ahead (l 44)
6   prestigious (ll 45–46)
7   in aid of (l 46)
8   scholarships (l 62)

Passage **b**
1   a lightning visit (l 1)
2   jackpot (l 10)
3   working out at (ll 14–15)
4   a chat show (ll 21–22)
5   fee (l 22)
6   showroom (ll 32–33)

Passage **c**
1   row (l 1)
2   urged (l 9)
3   absurd (l 16)
4   deprived (ll 20–21)
5   gives in (l 24)
6   overpays (l 27)

Use of English

A Finish each of the following sentences in such a way that it means the same as the sentence printed before it.

EXAMPLE: That table is so heavy that he can't lift it.
That table is too ....
ANSWER: *That table is too heavy for him to lift.*

1 Other guests will fork out £7,000 for a double ticket.
A double ticket ....

2 The meal ticket includes a family snapshot with the Prince and Princess.
A family snapshot ....

3 I'm sure they have no idea this kind of thing is going on.
They can't ....

4 Film stars are expected to attend.
It ....

5 Its organisers hope to raise £1,400,000.
£1,400,000 ....

6 Joan Collins earned £85,930 in five hours.
Five hours ....

7 Joan collected £20,000 for presenting a cheque to a pools winner.
£20,000 ....

8 First she made a ten-minute appearance on a chat show.
The first ....

9 They'll be forced to pay £65 a year if the government gives in.
Should ....

10 Millions of people will be shocked at this handout.
Shock ....

B For each of the sentences below, write a new sentence as similar as possible in meaning to the original sentence, but using the word given in **bold** letters. This word **must not be altered** in any way.

EXAMPLE: It wasn't my intention to frighten you.
mean
ANSWER: *I didn't mean to frighten you.*

1 The rent-a-royal plan has infuriated locals.
furious
....

2 They reckon Charles and Diana are being exploited.
opinion
....

3 Stars such as Bob Hope are expected to attend.
it
....

4 The amount of money raised caused great concern.
anxious
....

5 She slammed the 'hard sell' of Charles and Diana as 'not appropriate or polite'.
grounds
....

6 She earns £1,000 a minute in her role as superbitch Alexis.
playing
....

7 She made a ten-minute appearance on a chat show.
lasted
....

8 Last call was at the Hilton Hotel to draw a winning lottery ticket.
thing
....

9 A row has erupted over Selina Scott's new contract.
caused
....

10 The BBC overpays its prima donnas.
worth
....

Oral and written practice

Communication activity
Your teacher will ask you to look at a communication activity (2, 5, 8, 10, 12 or 15) at the back of the book. Each activity is part of a newspaper story. You will read out your part of the story to the others in your group and also listen to the other parts of the story read out by each of the other group members. By asking and answering questions, try to put the various parts of the story into their proper sequence. When you have done this, try to decide why *Back to Square One* is a suitable title for the story.

Picture discussion
Look at the photograph below and answer the questions which follow.

1 Describe the man in the picture.
2 What do you think he might be saying?
3 Why do you think he is carrying so much cash?
4 Do you think certain jobs are overpaid? If so, which ones?
5 Are people more materialistic now than in the past? If so, why?

Written work
1 You have just read the two articles entitled *£85,000 In a Day for Joan*, and *Storm Over Selina's Pay* in a daily newspaper and feel you must write a letter of protest to the editor, expressing your point of view on the subject. (about 200 words)
2 Write a composition on the following topic: 'The more you have, the less you are.' (about 350 words)

Test 1   Units 1–5   (30 minutes)

Choose the word or phrase which best completes each sentence. Indicate your answer by putting the letter A, B, C or D in the space in each sentence.

1 The idea of monarchy is often mixed .... religion.
   A out with   B up with   C with   D up in
2 Before the first public performance, the play was .... for five weeks.
   A repeated   B practised   C rehearsed   D put on
3 An extra-terrestrial is a(n) .... from another world.
   A life   B being   C been   D existence
4 I thought he was rather cold at first, but he .... to be quite friendly.
   A turned over   B turned up   C turned after   D turned out
5 It is said that the Queen .... many people's idea of perfection.
   A impersonates   B presents   C profiles   D embodies
6 After the business dinner, he proposed a .... to the future success of the company.
   A wish   B drink   C toast   D prediction
7 The international football match was .... by the national anthems.
   A preceded   B proceeded   C foreshadowed   D foreseen
8 They have decided to .... the out-of-date rule.
   A relax   B release   C let go   D leave
9 I was .... by the secretary's loyalty to her boss, who had been convicted of fraud.
   A struck   B stroked   C infected   D affected
10 Everyone was rather surprised when the literary prize was won by a(n) .... writer.
   A hidden   B unclear   C dark   D obscure
11 A political system that requires total obedience to those in power is called ....
   A authoritative   B authoritarian   C authentic   D authorised
12 The political, economic and social system in the USA is .... the individual person's aim to own property.
   A fixed on   B directed by   C based upon   D placed upon
13 In the army, every man is supposed to know his ....
   A situation   B placement   C post   D place
14 In most underdeveloped countries, many people survive by .... a meagre existence from the land.
   A wresting   B wrestling   C tearing   D forcing
15 By trying to reform the system of taxation, the new government has .... itself quite a problem.
   A made   B set   C put   D placed
16 In the army, insubordination is not ....
   A tolerated   B carried   C supported   D accustomed
17 There is no country which has a social system completely .... with the democratic ideal.
   A regular   B constant   C conforming   D consistent
18 In the late 1960s, there was a .... away from materialism.
   A style   B trend   C direction   D fashion
19 For a military system to be effective, democratic ideas must go ....
   A by the board   B overboard   C over the border   D on board
20 He makes me sick when he .... his money.
   A flaunts   B shows   C displays   D fleeces

21 It's rude to try to .... other people's secrets.
   A dig away   B dig down   C dig into   D dig in
22 Children born to wealthy families are said to be born with a silver ....
   in their mouth.
   A fork   B knife   C lollipop   D spoon
23 Economists often cannot .... for the fluctuations in currency values.
   A explain   B reason   C account   D reckon
24 If you're going for a walk in the country, it would be a good idea to wear
   .... clothes.
   A reasonable   B reasoned   C sensitive   D sensible
25 Bosses often hate .... shoulders with ordinary workers.
   A pressing   B frictioning   C touching   D rubbing
26 He only decided to marry her because she was well- ....
   A away   B off   C on   D under
27 The badly injured man .... to the telephone.
   A crept   B crawled   C slithered   D somersaulted
28 After drinking six pints of beer and six double whiskies, he had a severe
   .... the next morning.
   A hangover   B headpain   C headtap   D wooden mouth
29 She thought she'd got it .... when she married a millionaire.
   A fixed   B comfortably   C made   D away
30 The best clothes are the ones that don't ....
   A backdate   B date back   C update   D date
31 Gourmets are .... about the food they eat.
   A special   B particular   C painful   D delicate
32 He is not very articulate; he has trouble .... a sentence together.
   A wording   B hanging   C stringing   D binding
33 Arrogant people are often .... to other people's feelings.
   A oblivious   B forgetful   C unconcerned   D unconscious
34 In a state of extreme depression, he did .... himself.
   A away with   B down with   C off with   D over with
35 He's an expert .... that subject.
   A on   B about   C for   D with
36 If you pass the Proficiency examination, it will help your future work
   ....
   A hopes   B outlooks   C prospects   D perspectives
37 Aristocratic children are generally more ....
   A self-esteemed   B self-assured   C self-insured   D self-estimated
38 The class .... of French, Germans, Swiss, South Americans and
   Japanese.
   A consists   B composes   C comprises   D contains
39 If you live alone in a big city, you might have a sense of ....
   A insulation   B isolation   C insularity   D intrusion
40 Everything the Royal Family has is due to a(n) .... of birth.
   A chance   B opportunity   C privilege   D accident
41 His seven children and two ex-wives are proving to be a financial ....
   to him.
   A burden   B load   C charge   D debt
42 He tried to .... he would pass the exam by cheating.
   A assure   B empower   C ensure   D enable
43 I had to fork .... more than I expected to the tax authorities last year.
   A away   B out   C through   D in
44 The only way to make that shop reduce its prices is to .... it.
   A embargo   B refuse   C bypass   D boycott

45 They are hoping to .... a lot of money for charity.
   A organise   B bring up   C rise   D raise
46 Scholarships are provided for .... students.
   A deserving   B deserved   C meriting   D merited
47 The amount of money some Yuppies .... seems immoral.
   A win   B gain   C bring   D earn
48 When the winning lottery ticket was .... , nobody claimed it.
   A drawn   B decided   C pulled   D taken
49 When the redundancies were announced, a .... erupted.
   A discussion   B row   C quarrel   D temper
50 In the .... of the latest developments, we have decided to alter our
   plans.
   A consequence   B result   C light   D view

Unit 6

Tennis under Threat

Reading comprehension

Read the following passage, and then answer the questions which follow it.

I have seen John McEnroe's detestable tantrums and watched as Ilie Nastase's temper exploded. Yesterday, here at the same tennis court where Boris Becker honed the talent that took him to the Wimbledon singles title earlier this month, I was horror-struck at the legacy they have left us.

I stood and stared as one girl, eyes ablaze with anger, strode around the net to the other end of the court. In perfect English, she raged: "Where is the mark? Where? Where?" With her outsize racket she tapped her rival on the shoulder to demand, more furiously than before: "Do you speak English OK? I don't care what the umpire says. I want to see the mark." The girl with fury in her heart was just 11 years old. Even sadder was the sight of her parents joining in the argument, encouraging their daughter to remonstrate.

The belief that anarchy and dissident behaviour can have as much to do with creating a career in tennis as the possession of a strong serve and a good forehand seems to be common-place nowadays. The world of junior tennis is just a scaled-down version of the professional circuit and the pressures of competition, the insatiable demand to win, fuelled by starry-eyed parents and ambitious coaches, could be seen here without searching too hard. These youngsters daydream of the day they could stand where 17-year-old Becker stood, surrounded in glory, on Wimbledon's Centre Court less than three weeks ago.

When little Hungarian Annamaria Foldenyi lost yesterday, and after her mother had loudly and ungraciously applauded two double faults as Czech girl Petra Kucova served for the match, she broke down and sobbed. Her father Istvan tried to comfort Annamaria. But she just waved him away. She was inconsolable. Only after weeping pitifully for fully three minutes did she find it within herself to offer her opponent a half-hearted handshake. I spoke with Mr Foldenyi, who, in less emotional circumstances, is probably a rational man. Yesterday, for

him, was not a celebration of sport;
60 it was a rung for his daughter to
climb, and he was unhappy that she
should lose her footing. "We are
very fond of this sport and we want
to give something to our daughter,"
65 he said. Almost certainly, that
something is a place in the million-
dollar world of professional tennis.

Winnie Wooldridge, once ranked
No. 2 in Britain and here as captain
70 of the British girls' team, lamented:
"Tennis is not really a sport now;
it's a business—and they start doing
the business side very young. I have
even questioned if I'm doing the
75 right thing by being involved at all.
But I'm pigheaded enough, in a
way, to feel maybe I can make a
contribution. You've got to want to
hit a tennis ball in the first place, and
80 looking around at some of the kids
here it looks as if that's the last thing
they want to do."

The International Tennis Federation recently voted to discontinue
85 this year international tournaments
for under-12s and to outlaw under-
14s from the professional circuit.

They are concerned about too many
players becoming "burned out" by
90 too much tennis, too soon, like
Tracy Austin. Many of the youngsters here this week look like refugees from a field hospital, with one
or both knees heavily strapped.
95 There seems much wisdom in the
ITF's plan to abolish international
competition at under-12 level—
even though that plan might have to
be shelved for another 12 months.
100 Jack Chargelegue, chairman of the
European Tennis Association's
Under-21 Committee, explained
that the ETA are in the middle of a
contract with the Walt Disney Orga-
105 nisation that promotes junior tennis
under the banner of the Sport Goofy
Championship, embracing the
tournament here and in Florida in
the autumn. "There is much for us
110 to learn and much work to do. I
would like to see some scientific
research on the subject. But yes,
parents and coaches are very
dangerous. Educating them is the
115 main problem. They all think they
have a little Borg or Navratilova."

(From the *Daily Mail*)

1 Explain the phrase 'honed the talent' (lines 5–6).
2 What is 'the legacy' referred to in line 8?
3 What evidence is there in the passage of young tennis players' attitudes to authority and sporting behaviour?
4 What are 'starry-eyed parents' (line 35)?
5 What would the 'less emotional circumstances' (lines 56–57) be?
6 What does 'it' (line 60) refer to?
7 What is the meaning of 'a rung for his daughter to climb' (lines 60–61)?
8 What does Winnie Wooldridge feel her role in tennis should be?
9 What does 'that' (line 81) refer to?
10 What does 'They' (line 88) refer to?
11 Explain the phrase 'Many of the youngsters . . . look like refugees from a field hospital' (lines 91–93).
12 According to the passage, why can't international tennis at under-twelve level be abolished immediately?
13 In what way does Jack Chargelegue feel it is necessary to educate parents and coaches?
14 Summarise, in a paragraph of 70–100 words, what the passage says about the negative aspects of junior tennis.

Use of English

A Fill each of the numbered blanks in the following passage with **one** suitable word.

Pro tennis is currently suffering .... (1) the age-old problem of the rich .... (2) richer and the .... (3) getting poorer. Again, ... (4) must be stressed that not all things are relative. One need not spare too many tears .... (5) a young player of twenty-two who is earning .... (6) $60,000 a year, even allowing that an athlete's life is short and that tennis players generally pay their own travelling and lodging .... (7). These can knock $30,000 a year .... (8) anyone's income if they play up .... (9) forty weeks during the seemingly endless season. But with racket manufacturers selling less (.................... (10) surprising considering how much longer a graphite racket will .... (11) compared .... (12) the traditional wood model) it is more interesting to .... (13) which names are playing without endorsements rather than .... (14) who are. As far as Jimmy Connors and his Wilson T 2000 racket are .... (15), love rather .... (16) money is paramount. Connors is about the only person who can play with the thing and Wilson have long since given .... (17) hope of selling .... (18) to the public. They .... (19) refuse to pay Connors for using it. .... (20) offers rivalling the $600,000 a year Dunlop pay McEnroe, Connors refuses to part company with his steel-framed racket.

B For each of the sentences below, write a new sentence as similar as possible in meaning to the original sentence, but using the word given in **bold** letters. This word **must not be altered** in any way.

    EXAMPLE: It wasn't my intention to frighten you.
             mean
    ANSWER: *I didn't mean to frighten you.*

1 I have watched as Ilie Nastase's temper exploded.
    lost
    ....

2 I was horror-struck at the legacy they have left us.
    inherited
    ....

3 I don't care what the umpire says.
    couldn't
    ....

4 The pressures of competition could be seen here without searching too hard.
    need
    ....

5 She broke down and sobbed.
    tears
    ....

6 Only after weeping for several minutes did she shake her opponent's hand.
    when
    ....

7 Tennis is not really a sport now; it's a business.
    more
    ....

8   They recently voted to outlaw under-fourteens from the professional
    circuit.
    illegal

    ....

9   There is a plan to abolish international competition at under-twelve level.
    away

    ....

10 Parents and coaches are dangerous
    comes

Oral and written practice

Picture discussion
Look at the photograph below and answer the questions which follow.

1   What do you think is happening in the photograph?
2   If this photograph appeared in a newspaper, what headline would you give
    it?
3   Why do you think the tennis player is behaving in this way?
4   Have you ever behaved, or been tempted to behave, like him?
5   Why do you think this sort of behaviour is becoming more common?

Discussion topic

In groups, discuss the following points:

Sport in general has a more aggressive element nowadays. If a professional tennis player cannot control his temper during a match, the match should be stopped and his/her opponent declared the winner.

Parents who put great pressure on their children to be successful in sport do it to compensate for their own inadequacies and failures.

Children who are put under too much pressure to achieve success suffer both mentally and physically.

Written work

1   Write a composition (about 350 words) on the following topic: 'Sport is too commercialised nowadays.'
2   Write a description of a sportsman/sportswoman that you particularly admire. (about 250 words).

Unit 7

Clough Blasts Royal Hunters

Reading comprehension

The following text has been broken up into five parts, which have then been mixed up. Decide what the correct sequence should be.

a

"They looked too daft to laugh at when they were sitting on it.

"How can you have a Royal society to prevent cruelty to animals—or some of them—when Prince Charles goes hunting, and Prince Philip shooting?

"It's nonsense. And if you put Prince Charles in a room with me, he couldn't argue his way out of it".

But blood sports supporter Brian Toon of the Masters of Foxhounds Association doesn't believe hunting is about to end.

"The RSPCA won't do it—nor will the Labour Party, who should have learned their lesson at the last general election," he says.

"There are five and a half million people who take part in hunting, shooting and fishing—and that's a very big lobby to upset."

On cruelty Mr Toon says: "Hounds kill the fox within seconds. It is not torn apart alive."

b

Blood sports are barbaric and insensitive and should be banned by law.

That's the hard-hitting message Brian Clough has for our hunting Royals, Premier Margaret Thatcher and fellow soccer heroes Jimmy Hill and Jackie Charlton in 1986.

Following the Sunday Mirror's Save Our Countryside campaign, Britain's most controversial football manager believes the destruction of wildlife must become the year's burning issue.

He says: "The hunters tell themselves they belong to an elite. Well, thank God it is . . . because if we all behaved like them there wouldn't be anything walking, crawling, standing or even living on this island within a month.

"The countryside isn't run for the benefit of the hunting set. It belongs to everybody—just like fresh air. The hunters can be stopped."

His hatred for fox hunting, stag hunting, hare coursing and shooting was revealed recently when his Nottingham Forest team were staying in a New Forest hotel before a match against Southampton.

c

He was approached by two men to contribute to a charity.

Cloughie put his hand in his pocket and asked where the cash was going.

"I expected them to say underprivileged kids or whatever, but one of them said 'It's for the fox hunt'. I said two words to them—and the second was 'off'."

Clough's stand against blood sports is now backed by the RSPCA and the Labour Party—who have promised to outlaw fox-hunting if Neil Kinnock gets to 10 Downing Street.

Clough says: "If the Royal Family abandoned it, 50 per cent of the morons who hunt would pack it in immediately—and the rest wouldn't be far behind.

d

"There's something the matter with a society where we have to inflict pain on things.

"When I was a young bloke—I admit it—I used to shoot pheasants.

"But as you age and mature, your feelings change. Or they should. I live out in the country—and pheasants sit at the bottom of the garden eating my tulips.

"But I couldn't shoot one of them now to save my life."

Soccer has its own blood sports fans, including TV pundit and Managing Director of Charlton Athletic Jimmy Hill, and former Newcastle United manager Jack Charlton.

Brian says: "Mr Charlton . . . well, what can I say? I just wish every fox in the country could run as fast as he did when he left Newcastle."

Clough believes the Government must act. "It's time for some tough decisions on blood sports," he says. "But Mrs Thatcher daren't do it—because it's the Tories' own people involved.

"At last, the RSPCA have come down off the fence.

e

"But if the Royals don't stop soon, I'm going to get up a petition to shoot corgis. What would they think about that? They're animals too."

Clough says Prince Charles is moving in the right direction. Since his marriage, Charles no longer shoots—and goes fox hunting less often.

"I think he is being influenced by Princess Diana," says Brian.

"She can't show as much affection for children as she does and not show a pang of conscience for beautiful animals.

"She's not a woman who would get pleasure from grouse being shot for so-called sport.

"She wouldn't be happy at stag hunting—where a magnificent animal is chased to exhaustion, attacked by dogs and then has its throat slit.

"As for fox hunting, the mentality of the bloody people who do it is beyond me.

"And take hare coursing. I can't understand these bloody villains who take a hare from a bag, set it loose and let dogs race against one another to kill it.

(From the *Sunday Mirror*)

44

Vocabulary

A Find words or phrases in the text which correspond to the following definitions.

a
1 stop
2 on the point of
3 participate
4 annoy; make angry
5 pulled to pieces violently

b
1 uncivilised; very cruel
2 causing argument; arousing strong opinions
3 social group considered to be superior or special
4 moving slowly along the ground
5 organised

c
1 give money
2 disadvantaged
3 supported
4 make illegal
5 gave up

d
1 hurt physically
2 become older and wiser
3 supporters
4 person whose opinion is often asked for; expert
5 take the necessary steps

e
1 written document signed by a large number of people
2 doubtfully or wrongfully named
3 pursued
4 cut open
5 wicked/evil people

B Explain the meaning of the following words and phrases taken from the text

a
1 too daft to laugh at (ll 1–2)
2 were sitting on [the fence] (ll 2–3)
3 he couldn't argue his way out of it (ll 13–15)
4 should have learned their lesson (ll 24–25)
5 lobby (ll 32–33)

b
1 banned (l 3)
2 hard-hitting (l 4)
3 fellow soccer heroes (ll 8–9)
4 burning issue (l 19)
5 the hunting set (l 32)

c
1 or whatever (ll 8–9)
2 stand (l 14)
3 morons (l 25)
4 pack it in (l 26)
5 the rest wouldn't be far behind (ll 27–28)

d
1 There's something the matter with (ll 1–2)
2 bloke (l 6)
3 to save my life (ll 16–17)
4 tough (l 34)
5 come down off the fence (ll 42–43)

e
1 get up (l 3)
2 is moving in the right direction (ll 9–10)
3 a pang of conscience (l 20)
4 is beyond me (ll 35–36)
5 set it loose (ll 40–41)

Use of English

A Finish each of the following sentences in such a way that it means the same as the sentence printed before it.

> EXAMPLE: That table is so heavy that he can't lift it.
>   That table is too ....
> ANSWER: *That table is too heavy for him to lift.*

1   If we all behaved like that, there wouldn't be anything living on this island.
    Were ....

2   The hunters can be stopped.
    It ....

3   I said two words to them – and the second was 'off'.
    'Off' ....

4   The Labour Party will outlaw foxhunting if Neil Kinnock gets to Downing Street.
    Providing ....

5   If the Royals don't stop soon, I'm going to get up a petition to shoot corgis.
    Unless ....

6   The mentality of the people who do it is beyond me.
    I ....

7   I couldn't shoot a pheasant to save my life.
    The last thing ....

8   I wish every fox in the country could run as fast as he did.
    If ....

9   How can you have a Royal society to prevent cruelty to animals when the Royal Family go hunting and shooting?
    I find ....

10   There are five and a half million people who take part in hunting, shooting and fishing.
    The number ....

B Fill each of the blanks in the following passage with a suitable phrase.

> EXAMPLE: .... tennis in that heat, you would have been exhausted.
> ANSWER: *If you had played . . .*

Unless you have experienced the chase, most huntsmen strongly maintain that you .... (1) what excites them. The hunting fraternity claims that nothing else in life can quite equal the pounding joy of 'chasing Charlie Fox'.

'A good run can never really .... (2) in words,' a regular huntsman told me. They prefer not to use their names because .... (3) retribution from anti-hunting hardliners. 'Hunting can leave you literally trembling. There is no experience to compare with being at the front of a hunt, steaming across the countryside. Clearing large fences on a huge horse is a unique sensation. You feel as .... (4) flying.'

Modern hunting first took .... (5) nineteenth century when sportsman Hugo Meynell founded the modern

English chase. Very quickly, it developed into a national upper-class sport. It is this lingering posh image that still irritates town dwellers, who .... (6) solely as a privileged preserve. This is a myth. Hunting is a country sport and most of its supporters and followers are working-class folk. Although costly, it is always popular with the locals.

But there is also a practical side to hunting: controlling the fox. This animal, despite his glamorous appearance, appealing eyes, ears and distinctive brush, is vermin. He is also a prolific breeder and a quite vicious killer. He has the .... (7) breaking into henhouses – not to eat the birds, merely to slaughter. He has been known to attack sheep and tear their backs out. Hunters will tell you that part of their role .... (8) fox population under control while not ex-terminating them totally. They are against the shooting of foxes by farmers largely because it is impractical: if hunting .... (9) in Britain there would be an 'open season' on foxes. Hunting people are keen to dispel the idea that their hounds tear the fox apart. They main-tain the dogs go .... (10) jugular vein and he is dead when they pounce on him.

Oral and written practice

Picture discussion
Look at the cartoon below and answer the questions which follow.

1 What's going to happen? Why?
2 Describe the two people, including their clothes and what they are carrying.
3 Do you think this cartoon symbolises anything?
4 What do you think of hunting as a sport?

Discussion topic

Below are four passages, all on the subject of hunting. You will be asked to look at one of them and comment on the content and possible source of the text, the sort of person the writer or speaker is likely to be, and, where appropriate, what the purpose of the passage is. You might also agree or disagree with the content – if so, say why.

a

"We had a marvellous gallop, a really beautiful time and, although we would have preferred not to have dug that fox out, it was something that had to be done. I can assure you that if we had left that fox there someone would have come along later with a gas canister to kill it and maybe others. Which was better?

"You can see we are a complete cross-section of the community, something the Antis never seem to accept. They haven't affected us this time, but they are a darned menace. They do terrible things, you know. They think they are above the law and this is why we have to have the police here."

b

"One particular hunt killed 26 lambs in one afternoon. The hunting season is only two months old and already there have been a few pet-killing incidents.

"The reported cases are much-loved pets, but we know there are hundreds of incidents where strays are killed.

"If a gang of youths regularly invaded villages, charged down the streets, trampled through gardens and private land terrorising people and indiscriminately killing pets, questions would be asked in the House of Commons."

c

The dedication on the arched gravestone read:

MERLE
1854–75

There had never been a formal grave with a defined boundary, but the Duke had ordered the keepers of the time to keep the ground clear of any growth which might obscure the headstone. Now, a tangle of ivy and grasses concealed the lower part of the headstone, right up to the date, and a holly bush, rooted amongst the bones of the horse, formed a natural tribute to the animal.

The labrador cocked his leg and marked the stone. The gamekeeper let him. He did not like foxhunting. He thought it was cruel.

d

> The Duke shot grouse on his three moors on alternate weeks, Friday, Saturday and Monday, and when he was not shooting on his own moors, he was touring the north of England and Scotland shooting on somebody else's. It was a full time job, travelling and shooting, through August, September and for the first two weeks in October. He had a change for one week in September when he went over to France to shoot partridge on Count Mauriac's estate, and after the last shoot in October, he took a fortnight's holiday on his estate in Ireland to recuperate in time for the pheasant shooting in November.

Written work

1   In about 350 words, continue the following story:
    I was approaching the village when the hunt suddenly came across the fields. As soon as the dogs saw us, they started baying. Then they attacked.

2   'Hunting – the unspeakable in pursuit of the uneatable.' Discuss. (about 350 words)

Unit 8

Survival of the Thickest?

Reading comprehension

Read the following passage, and then decide whether the statements which follow it are true or false. Be prepared to justify your answers. If you feel that there is not enough evidence to justify true or false, put a question mark.

SCIENCE teacher John McIntyre has quit—and sent his bosses a pictorial protest to draw his reasons to their attention.

5 He sketched a cartoon of children fighting, drinking, smoking and even using a gun in the classroom.

"Discipline has broken down completely," said John, 23. "I just can't face any more, I can't carry on teaching in such 10 conditions."

John sent copies of his cartoon to the headmaster and all 12 governors of Amery Hill comprehensive 15 school, Alton, Hants.

Four years ago a 16-year-old girl fired a shotgun in a classroom there. A court heard she had threatened to 20 kill a teacher.

Now John claims that in 18 months at the school he has witnessed more violence, vandalism and crime among 25 its 800 pupils.

"I've had my car tyres slashed," he said at his home in Rake, near Liss, Hants. "Teachers have been attack-30 ed in the classroom.

"Waste bins are set on fire and kids swear at the teachers. A flick-knife has been confiscated and por-35 nographic magazines are left in the library.

"Once a boy kicked down a classroom door.

"And prefects took 40 another boy to the police when he attacked a pupil.

"I know of cases where boys have left money in the school, but have broken in 45 during the night to pick it up.

"Then they claimed the money from the school, saying it was stolen by some-50 one else.

"There's no back-up from the staff in trying to discipline the kids.

55 "The headmaster doesn't believe in corporal punishment and things are too soft. I feel the cane should be brought back."

John, whose resignation 60 takes effect from the end of next term, added: "I haven't got another job to go to. I don't know what I'm going to do."

65 Amery Hill headmaster Mr Alan Parry-Jones, who joined the school a year ago, said: "It's an unusual way of resigning. But I don't wish to 70 comment further."

Mr John Dixon, parents' representative on the board of governors, said: "There are always difficulties with 75 discipline in schools. But Amery Hill has done very well.

"There have been complaints from time to time, 80 but no more than in any other school."

A spokesman for Hampshire education department said: "Mr McIntyre's car-85 toon is witty, well-drawn, but totally unrealistic.

"Discipline at Amery Hill is good, and is not regarded as a problem."

(From the *News of the World*)

1 John McIntyre didn't leave his job of his own accord.
2 The cartoon depicts a typical lesson in the school.
3 The cartoon was intended to indicate to his employers why he resigned.
4 McIntyre sent the cartoon to his boss and the local education department.
5 Many pupils at Amery Hill are potential criminals.
6 A female pupil once took a deadly weapon into school.
7 McIntyre's car has been vandalised.
8 Pornographic magazines can be obtained from the library.
9 Some pupils have committed burglaries at the school.
10 Police were asked to come to the school to stop pupils fighting.
11 The headmaster has never caned anyone in his life.
12 McIntyre feels the staff could do more to support each other.
13 McIntyre will be on the dole when he leaves his job.
14 The authorities believe that discipline at Amery Hill is adequate.
15 It seems that the authorities will conduct an investigation into Amery Hill.

Vocabulary

A Find words or phrases in the passage which correspond to the following
definitions.

1 collapsed; disintegrated
2 continue
3 seen
4 taken away (as a punishment)
5 entered illegally

6 get; collect
7 there's not enough discipline
8 becomes legally valid
9 giving up one's job
10 amusing; humorous

B Explain the meaning of the following words and phrases taken from the
passage

1 quit (l 2)
2 to draw his reasons to
   their attention (ll 3–4)
3 sketched (l 5)
4 face (l 9)
5 slashed (l 27)

6 flick-knife (l 33)
7 prefects (l 39)
8 back-up (l 51)
9 corporal punishment (l 55)
10 spokesman (l 82)

Use of English

A Finish each of the following sentences in such a way that it means the same
as the sentence printed before it.

EXAMPLE: That table is so heavy that he can't lift it.
        That table is too ....
ANSWER: *That table is too heavy for him to lift.*

1 He sketched children fighting, drinking and smoking.
   His sketch ....

2 Discipline has broken down completely.
   There has ....

3 McIntyre has witnessed more violence among the pupils.
   McIntyre has witnessed an ....

4   I've had my car tyres slashed.
    My ....

5   Kids swear at the teachers.
    The teachers ....

6   I feel the cane should be brought back.
    I feel it ....

7   The present headmaster joined the school a year ago.
    It ....

8   I don't wish to comment further.
    I have ....

9   McIntyre's cartoon is witty, but totally unrealistic.
    In spite ....

10 Discipline at Amery Hill is not regarded as a problem.
    We ....

B   Fill each of the blanks in the following passage with a suitable phrase.

EXAMPLE: .... tennis in that heat, you would have been exhausted.
ANSWER: *If you had played . . .*

A Letter to the Editor

I read the arguments against caning with a great ....
.... (1) interest, both as a parent and ....
.... (2) in a comprehensive school. In theory, I agree with every
word; .... (3) least five years
since I strapped anyone. However, we do not live in an ideal world, and children
in school do not behave as they do at home, nor ....
.... (4) teachers as people, but rather as fair game.

Today I broke .... (5) between
two fifteen-year-old boys – after one ....
.... (6) the other in the eye when he was on the ground. I left it at a 'good
talking-to', and the boys shaking hands. However, when the fighters are National
Front members beating up coloured kids, a talking-to is water off a duck's back.
I'm a five-foot tall woman. What ....
.... (7) about a sixteen-year-old youth, five feet ten tall, who follows me down
the corridor mouthing obscenities? Or the lad who put on his football boots and
walked over my car the first ....
... (8) school? Tell them they're naughty boys? Attempt to slap them? Ask the
headmaster to strap them with all due ceremony, and the punishment book? And
if he won't, have they got ....
... (9) it?

The strap is used very rarely in my school – but it's there, the last ditch against
anarchy when we're up .... (10)
have no desire or intention to fit in, to work, to learn, or to conform to acceptable
standards of civilised behaviour.

Oral and written practice

Picture discussion
Look at the cartoon below and answer the questions which follow.

1　What activities described in the passage at the beginning of the unit can you see in the cartoon?
2　Where's the teacher in the cartoon?
3　How does this behaviour compare with behaviour in schools in your country?
4　How do you think you would react if you were a teacher new to this school?
5　What do you think causes such behaviour?

Discussion topic
Below are three extracts from newspaper articles on student behaviour problems in secondary schools. Read them, taking note of the differing points of view on the subject.

A TOP headmaster has called for schools to set up sin-bins where unruly pupils can be dumped and allowed to play cards all day.

Mr X said in each school there was a small minority of pupils of the kind he calls "The Unteachables". They cannot be taught simply because they refuse to study.

He wants them rounded up and separated from the rest of the pupils to avoid disruption of classes.

Then they would be placed in a classroom, or even another building, where they would be allowed a free rein to do what they wanted.

Strain
"The families seem to think it's up to us to do something about their behaviour. But my teachers are under enormous strain trying to deal with these children, while at the same time trying to teach the rest of the class."

Mr X's controversial solution to classroom anarchy comes in the wake of a damning survey on comprehensive schools in which two-thirds of parents questioned wanted all-in education scrapped.

The parents blamed growing violence, lack of discipline and political bias in teaching for poor standards.

Mr X, 49, added: "I am not a defeatist, but there is simply nothing we can do about these disruptive children other than remove them from the scene.

Escape

Mr X, a firm supporter of the comprehensive system, said: "My friends tell me I'm playing into the hands of the pro-grammar school lobby. I'm aware that some people may think my views are a little controversial, but I believe if there is a problem you should talk about it."

Former Education Minister Dr Rhodes Boyson—known for his disciplinarian views—condemned Mr X's proposal.

"It would provide an escape hatch for every child who didn't want to learn," he said.

"It would place a value on being disruptive and would set a dangerous precedent."

The National Union of Teachers also expressed dismay.

An NUT spokesman said: "We agree there is a small minority of disruptive children and that it might be a positive step to move them into a special class or disruptive unit for a limited period.

"But they would need specialist help from teachers experienced in tackling severe behavioural problems in children.

"It would be wrong to leave them to their own devices."

(From the *Sunday Express*)

(From the *Daily Mirror*)

Teachers who are already on the sharp end of Government cuts claim their job is being made far worse by parents who just don't care.

In many cases there is no discipline in the home—and no cooperation with the school, say teachers.

Teachers all over the country are reporting an increase in the number of mothers and fathers who are shirking their responsibilities.

And there is concern over the increasing number of parents who physically attack teachers for disciplining their children.

What is alarming is the fact that violence and vandalism is creeping into primary schools.

SCHOOL DISCIPLINE

The teachers couldn't control bullying or vandalism or smoking. The boys were cheeky to them and the teachers didn't know how to cope. I just wasn't happy with the way the school was run.

Discipline was quite good at my school, even though we're in a rough area. We had the cane, although I never knew anyone who got it. I think it's a good idea, even if it's just a threat.

We had detentions mostly—trouble is they're silly, they don't work. You only had to stay behind half an hour and people used to muck about anyway. Detention never stopped me doing anything. The cane would have done.

I enjoyed school and I thought it was good. Mine was definitely stricter on discipline than most and I'm glad because if it hadn't been I don't think I'd have got through any exams, let alone 7 O-levels.

HOME DISCIPLINE

"My Mum used to thump me when I'd done wrong, which I think's okay. She wasn't always nagging: it was just "bonk!" and "don't do that again, or I'll tell your Dad!" She never did though—in fact sometimes she'd cover up for me. I was much more frightened of my dad and I could never talk to him. Still can't."

"I get on very well with both my parents. They were very strict with me over things like manners and what time I got home at night. I was a bit of a rebel between 14 and 16 so I resented it. But now I see the point of it all and I'm really grateful."

(From the *Daily Mirror*)

You are going to take part in a group discussion. Your teacher will tell you to speak for two minutes from one of the points of view given below. You will be allowed to make brief notes before the discussion. Use the information above and in the earlier parts of the unit to help you.

School discipline – what is the solution?

You are:

a secondary school teacher who is seriously thinking of leaving the profession after six years of service.

a parent who feels that schools do not 'discipline' children enough.

a professional education expert who feels that the problem has been exaggerated out of all proportion.

a secondary school pupil who feels that most teachers don't care about their pupils and therefore don't deserve any respect. You also think that most parents refuse to accept their responsibilities.

Written work

1   You are an experienced teacher at a state secondary school. One of your classes is going to be taken for the next two weeks by a trainee teacher as part of his/her teacher-training course. As certain members of this class tend to be rather disruptive and aggressive, you feel that it might be best to leave this new teacher a short letter, warning him/her of the possible problems and who the main offenders are likely to be. Write the letter. (about 200 words)
2   'There are three possible reasons for discipline problems: the teacher, the students and the institution.' Discuss. (about 350 words)

Unit 9

Theory X versus Theory Y

Reading comprehension

You will find after each of the following passages a number of statements, each with four suggested endings. Choose the answer which you think fits best.

First passage

THEORY X	THEORY Y
The average human being has an inherent dislike of work and will avoid it if he can.	15 The expenditure of physical and mental effort in work is as natural as play or rest.
5 Because of this human characteristic of dislike of work, most people must be coerced, controlled, directed, threatened with punishment to get them to put forth adequate effort toward the achievement of organiza-10 tional objectives.	External control and the threat of punishment are not the only means for 20 bringing about efforts toward organizational objectives. Man will exercise self-direction and self-control in the service of objectives to which he is committed.
	25 Commitment to objectives is a function of the rewards associated with their achievement.
The average human being prefers to be directed, wishes to avoid responsibility, has relatively little ambition, wants security above all.	The average human being learns, under proper conditions, not only to 30 accept but to seek responsibility.
	The capacity to exercise a relatively high degree of imagination, ingenuity, and creativity in the solution of organizational problems is widely, not nar-35 rowly, distributed in the population.
	Under the conditions of modern industrial life, the intellectual potentialities of the average human being are only partially utilized.

(From *The Human Side of Enterprise* by D. McGregor)

1   Theory X is
    A   traditional and progressive in character, while theory Y is essentially
        autocratic and participative.
    B   progressive and participative in character, while theory Y is essentially
        traditional and autocratic.
    C   traditional and autocratic in character, while theory Y is essentially
        progressive and participative.
    D   autocratic and progressive in character, while theory Y is essentially
        traditional and participative.

2   A teacher who adopts a teaching style consistent with theory X
    A   is more concerned with his students' potential for growth and develop-
        ment.
    B   believes the capacities of his students are vastly improvable.
    C   is more concerned with his students' behaviour as it is rather than with
        growth and development.
    D   will be constantly involved in change and innovation.

3   A teacher who adopts a teaching style consistent with theory Y
    A   believes that students will have to be manipulated, controlled and
        conditioned to get them to invest the necessary effort.
    B   can still be autocratic or permissive – according to the situational needs.
    C   will always be permissive with his students.
    D   will rarely be flexible in style.

4   According to theory Y, an average person today
    A   has a potent intellect.
    B   has unlimited intellectual capacities.
    C   is not tested intellectually.
    D   is not required to fulfil his intellectual potential.

5   The passage seems to be taken from:
    A   a newspaper report.
    B   an instruction leaflet intended for teachers.
    C   a textbook.
    D   a work of fiction.

Second passage

THEORY X

A theory X teacher will seek to compensate for his students' weaknesses and
deficiencies by adopting one of two teaching styles based on a carrot and
stick approach to motivation:
1. A hard approach. This involves coercing students to learn by using
teaching strategies that are essentially autocratic and teacher-centred.
These will enable him to discipline, control, punish, threaten and cajole
students, as well as to exercise constant surveillance over their work.
2. A soft approach. This involves coaxing students to learn by using
teaching strategies that are essentially permissive and student-centred.
These will enable him to reward, praise, blame, love and bribe students, as
well as to ensure that students' initiative is not stifled.
    Both these approaches are based on the assumption that students dislike
and will avoid learning, and must therefore be manipulated, controlled or

conditioned so as to get them to invest the necessary effort. It is true that
15 there is an essential difference between the task-centred and the human
relations-centred approaches, but the result is the same. Extrinsic motivation in the form of control or love is used as a vehicle to cause students to
work. Coercing a student to learn, however, will tend to lead to resistance,
apathy and minimum effort: coaxing a student to learn may well lead to
20 comfortable relationships in the classroom, but is unlikely to lead to
anything but the minimum effort in furthering learning objectives.

THEORY Y

A theory Y teacher is sometimes misrepresented as someone who believes
that students will work harder if left to their own devices, rather than firmly
led. This is as naive as it is untrue. Under the right conditions, many people
25 will find sufficient satisfaction in their work, and they will invest more effort
than if they are coerced or coaxed. Teachers, however, have to set up the
right conditions for this to happen, and it is here that a teacher-leader has to
exercise his great skill, experience and sensitivity. It is certainly not easy to
so structure a learning situation that students will obtain a sense of personal
30 achievement and personal growth. But, student motivation can be
harnessed by enriching the learning experience. In any case, intrinsic
motivation is considerably more powerful and sustaining, over a longer
period, than extrinsic motivation, and, furthermore, is more closely aligned
to the real aims of education and training.
35   A theory Y teacher regards his students as natural decision-makers and
problem-solvers, and he attempts to harness these potentialities by adopting
a style that is most likely to realize the learning objectives of the moment.
This demands a certain degree of flexibility of style, as well as a highly
developed sensitivity, so that the needs of students and task can be properly
40 explored and assessed. There is an indication that teachers working with
students whose achievement and attitudes are superior tend to be sensitive
enough to diagnose situation needs, able to match their diagnosis with
action, and flexible enough to change their style spontaneously and at will.
Less successful teachers, on the other hand, appear to be restricted to a
45 limited number of roles, and unable to vary their style from one situation to
another.

(From *The Management of Learning* by Professor I Davies)

6 A theory X teacher who adopts a hard approach does it
   A   to motivate his students to work.
   B   to force his students to work.
   C   because he's essentially autocratic.
   D   because he feels his students need punishing.

7 A theory X teacher who adopts a soft approach wants
   A   to have a friendly atmosphere in the classroom.
   B   his students to show minimum effort.
   C   his students to work hard.
   D   to bribe students to work.

8 A theory Y teacher believes that
   A   it is up to the teacher to create the appropriate conditions for learning to
        take place.

B a combination of extrinsic and intrinsic motivation is desirable.
C students will learn if they are left to their own devices.
D teachers have to be experienced and sensitive.

9 From the passage it can be assumed that
A a theory Y teacher has to be a motivator.
B a theory Y teacher has to change the existing system.
C a theory Y teacher will not believe in any methodology.
D a theory Y teacher believes that different methodologies are appropriate to different situations.

10 Successful teachers
A should be able to change their approach when the need arises.
B should only use a limited number of roles.
C always achieve their learning objectives.
D are spontaneous in approach.

Use of English

A Fill each of the numbered blanks in the following passage with **one** suitable word.

The two theories are essentially statements of .... (1) one person's influence .... (2) another person's behaviour is believed to take .... (3). Since our behaviour .... (4) teachers is usually consistent .... (5) the assumptions we .... (6) about students, the teaching style we .... (7) will broadly indicate .... (8) philosophy. This is particularly important because of .... (9) has been called 'the self-fulfilling prophecy'.

Self-fulfilling prophecy
When we make assumptions about our .... (10), they will often tend .... (11) behave in a way that is .... (12) with these assumptions. In other words, they .... (13) the prophecies we make about them. Students who are .... (14) as trouble-makers become trouble-makers, students who are viewed as .... (15) behave as failures. The self-fulfilling prophecy, of course, also .... (16) in the opposite direction. .... (17) who are regarded as able, mature, responsible and successful often behave in a .... (18) which vindicates our prediction. .... (19) is for this reason that teaching style is a matter of great importance. Style affects the .... (20) environment in which students learn.

B Finish each of the following sentences in such a way that it means the same as the sentence printed before it.

EXAMPLE: That table is so heavy that he can't lift it.
That table is too ....
ANSWER: *That table is too heavy for him to lift.*

1 The average human being wants security above all.
The principal ....

2 Man will exercise self-control in the service of objectives to which he is committed.
If man ....

3 The average human being learns not only to accept but also to seek responsibility.
Not only ....

4 These strategies will enable him to exercise constant surveillance over their work.
These strategies will make ....

5 Coercing a student to learn will lead to resistance, apathy and minimum effort.
Resistance ....

6 This is as naive as it is untrue.
This is both ....

7 Under the right conditions, many people will find sufficient satisfaction in their work.
If ....

8 Teachers have to set up the right conditions for this to happen.
It is up to ....

9 Student motivation can be harnessed by enriching the learning experience.
The way ....

10 Less successful teachers appear to be restricted to a limited number of roles.
It ....

Oral and written practice

Picture discussion
Look at the photograph below and answer the questions which follow.

1 What do you think the children in the picture are learning?
2 Do you think that the use of computers in education is closer to a theory X or theory Y approach?
3 Computers are becoming more and more popular in education. Can you think of any advantages a computer might have over a more traditional (i.e. teacher in front of class) system?
4 Have you ever used a computer?
5 Do you think that teachers will ever be completely replaced? Why/why not?

Discussion topic
In groups, decide which of these subjects should be compulsory for all pupils from the age of twelve:

Sport	Mathematics
Computer skills	History
Religion	Domestic science
A foreign language	Economics
Politics	Geography

Now compare your conclusions with other groups.

Written work
1 Write a description of the strictest teacher you ever had. (about 350 words)
2 Write a composition (about 350 words) on the following topic: 'Schools do not prepare a child for the outside world.'

Unit 10

Brains + Hard Work = Genius

Reading comprehension

Read the following passage, and then answer the questions which follow it.

HARRY Lawrence is a man with a message. He passionately believes that all parents can learn from the phenomenal academic success of his 13-year-old daughter, Ruth.

The enormity of Ruth's mathematical achievement at St. Hugh's College, Oxford, is difficult to grasp. In two years she completed a three year degree course, covering 17 topics in the past year while fellow students studied three or four.

Her work spanned a broad range, from number theory and logic on the pure side, over to general relativity and quantum mechanics in applied mathematics.

This meant that during her finals she was able to answer 11 or 12 questions on each of the eight papers compared to the four or five questions tackled by those normally consi-dered to be exceptional students.

By the end of the exams she had piled up so many marks that, had the marks of the next best student, Paul Ling, been taken from her total, she would still have walked away with a First. And this was in a year that Paul Ling's performance earned him a special com-mendation last awarded 20 years ago. Ruth Law-rence was commended alongside him.

Now, as Ruth prepares to study for a doctorate, her father insists the achievement could be mirrored by others. Mr. Lawrence has never made more than modest claims about his daughter's abil-ity. He admits only that she has a "good brain". Descriptions like genius and child prodigy he leaves to the Press.

The hub of his argu-ment is the belief that if Ruth were a genius, it would be genius born of 90 per cent effort. Ruth maintans an average eight-hour daily work schedule of mathematics study, working at a rate which has astonished her Oxford tutors.

But her father stresses that the study is entirely self-motivated through an insatiable appetite for her subject.

Ruth began reading starter books at four but in 12 months she de-veloped her reading abil-ity to that of a nine-year-old. By the time she started maths tuition at the age of five her parents had decided that school would be a waste of time.

Mr. Lawrence gave up his job as a computer consultant to concentrate on one-to-one teaching at home using ideas formu-lated by the Greek philo-sopher Socrates to lead Ruth on to her own dis-coveries through a sequ-ence of questions and

100 answers.

Harry Lawrence has never resorted to thumping out his strongly felt and controversial educa-
105 tional beliefs. But behind the gentle, bearded features of this 49-year-old former teacher, hides something of a revolu-
110 tionary academic with little time for the state education system.

Many of his educational theories were drawn
115 from his own school experiences. He said: "I could see what was wrong. They didn't even stretch you intellectually.
120 For many years I had to put up with the idea that you couldn't do anything early."

Later, as a teacher in a
125 London secondary modern school he saw frustrated youngsters waiting to leave school. "They were not working to-
130 wards any particular exam. The only reason they were there was because a piece of legislation said they had to go to
135 school," he said.

The observation leads him to argue for greater parental involvement in education. He said: "I am
140 arguing for parental supremacy. The educational system should think of itself as performing a service to the parents whose
145 children it is looking

after.

"Instead it likes to talk of giving a service to the child while cutting the
150 parent out. I think that's wrong. Your child is your future. The child is your immortal being.

"I think it's wrong for
155 educationists to say 'We know what should be done and we might let you have a say in it'. Education is a service.
160 The customers are the parents.

"I believe there is a big minority of parents who would like to go into
165 schools and take part in teaching. This way their children can benefit from the expert advice of teachers, and the one-to-
170 one relationship with a parent. Schools could surely provide that facility.

"Then there are some
175 parents who want to be responsible for their children's education. They shouldn't be impeded. My main theme is plural-
180 ity of education based on parents' decisions."

He is wary of predictions about Ruth's future since she has already built
185 up a solid depth of knowledge over a wide range of mathematical subjects. Her advantage is that she will be able to pick on
190 ideas that flourish in one subject and use them in

another. The disadvantage is that she likes ev-
195 erything, so she doesn't know which avenue to go down.

The father and daughter partnership—that is the best way to describe
200 them—intends to spend the next year deciding the course of Ruth's future studies which must involve original research for a Ph.D thesis.

This idea of breaking new ground is clearly exciting to both of them. Mr. Lawrence recalled
210 the French mathematician Evariste Galois who died from a duelling wound in 1832 at the age of 21.

"Before he died his work had been so important that it changed the course of maths. The group theories arising out
220 of his work form the basis for the latest atomic theory," he explained as his daughter raised a small point of contention.
225 Numerous debates over statements of fact are a constant feature of any conversation with Ruth and her father. Neither claim that Ruth would be another Galois, but Mr. Lawrence speaks of a "flowering" period in front of her to the age of
235 25 when he believes that the adult mind reaches the end of its creative period.

(From the *Yorkshire Post*)

1 In general terms, what is 'a man with a message'?
2 What do the expressions 'difficult to grasp' (line 13) and 'a broad range' (line 21) mean?
3 What does 'This' (line 27) refer to?
4 What does Ruth's father consider her motivation to be?
5 Why did Ruth's parents decide not to send her to school?

6   What was the basic principle underlying Ruth's education?
7   What do you understand by the phrase 'has never resorted to . . . educational beliefs' (lines 101–105)?
8   What does Harry Lawrence believe was wrong with his own education?
9   What does 'that' (line 150) refer to?
10 What is the facility referred to in line 173?
11 According to Ruth's father, what is her disadvantage?
12 What is the 'new ground' referred to in line 207?
13 What do you understand by 'a "flowering" period' (line 233)?
14 Summarise, in not more than 120 words, the ways in which Ruth has proved to be exceptional for her age.

Use of English

A   Fill each of the blanks in the following passage with a suitable phrase.

> EXAMPLE: .... tennis in that heat, you would have been exhausted.
> ANSWER: *If you had played . . .*

An Expert's View

At once, he was provocative. It was absolute balderdash, he said, to state that all are equal .... (1) as genetic laws existed. 'Gifted children' was a .... (2) define. They came from every class – there have been remarkable working-class geniuses. The Russians combed *all* schools for giftedness, and accusations of 'elitism' .... (3) a small minority. Intelligence wasn't measurable; it was a function, and .... (4) of education, as Jerome Bruner has said, ... (5) pursuit of potential. Potential for giftedness emerged in the attitude of the parents, and gifted children were not necessarily problems. Mr Armstrong maintained that children do not learn from each other .... (6) guided, helped, coached by people more knowledgeable, by intelligent adults who .... (7) in a position where they can learn how to learn.

How can we tell the gifted child? He can be the bored one at school, whom .... (8) to teach when faced with a class I.Q. range from seventy to a hundred and ten. Schools should aim to produce .... (9) excellence: professors of astronomy, computer experts and happy dustmen! Most of us, especially the English, accept under-achievement, but we .... (10) be stretched, for our best work is often done under stress.

B   For each of the sentences below, write a new sentence as similar as possible in meaning to the original sentence, but using the word given in **bold** letters. This word **must not be altered** in any way.

> EXAMPLE: It wasn't my intention to frighten you.
>   **mean**
> ANSWER: *I didn't mean to frighten you.*

1   She would still have walked away with a First.
    trouble
    ....

2   Ruth's work has astonished her Oxford tutors.
    astonishing
    ....

3   Ruth has an insatiable appetite for her subject.
    satisfied
    ....

4   Mr Lawrence gave up his job as a computer consultant.
    resigned
    ....

5   He has little time for the state educational system.
    opinion
    ....

6   The only reason they were there was because of a piece of legislation.
    if
    ....

7   Their children could benefit from the expert advice of teachers.
    beneficial
    ....

8   Some parents want to be responsible for their children's education.
    take
    ....

9   This idea is clearly exciting to both of them.
    they
    ....

10 The adult mind reaches the end of its creative period at twenty-five.
    over...

Oral and written practice

Discussion topic
Do you agree or disagree with the following statements?

Schools are incapable of giving a bright child a proper education. Parents should be allowed to take full responsibility for their children's education if they choose to do so.

Most school programmes don't stretch the above-average child intellectually. This can lead to boredom, and, ultimately, discipline problems.

Very bright children are often persecuted by their peers, and often have difficulty in making friends.

Schools should give as much consideration to gifted children as they do to those who are under-achieving.

Bright children from middle-class families have much more chance of succeeding than those from working-class families.

Picture discussion

Look at the picture below and answer these questions.

1 Describe the picture.
2 Do you think the scene inside the person's head symbolises stupidity, frustrated genius, or something else?
3 Do you think it is possible to be very intelligent, yet still do very badly at school? If so, explain why.
4 Which would you most like to be: a highly intelligent child or a child who is extremely gifted at sport? Why?
5 Which of the two examples in the previous question do you think would be most admired by their fellow students? Why?

Written work

1 Write a story which ends with the sentence: *You see, on the one hand you're expected to be clever and pass all your exams, yet on the other hand if you prove to be too exceptional, you're treated as an outsider.* (about 350 words)

2 Do you think that Harry Lawrence (in the passage at the beginning of this unit) has done the right thing in bringing up his daughter in such a way? Do you think she will ever be able to lead a normal life? What do you think of his ideas about education? Give your opinion on these things in about 350 words.

Test 2 Units 6–10 (30 minutes)

Choose the word or phrase which best completes each sentence. Indicate your answer by putting the letter A, B, C or D in the space in each sentence.

1 His will to win .... him to first place in the world tennis rankings.
   A induced   B boosted   C took   D brought

2 Some spectators were ....-struck at the tennis player's appalling behaviour.
   A fear   B scandal   C horror   D disgust

3 The .... of professional sportsmen hurling abuse at each other shocks some spectators.
   A sight   B view   C experience   D action

4 The belief that winning is the main thing seems to be .... nowadays.
   A mundane   B daily   C commonplace   D current

5 When she lost the match, she broke .... and sobbed.
   A down   B up   C in   D apart

6 Ambitious people often want to climb to the highest .... of their profession.
   A bars   B rungs   C stairs   D perches

7 He was climbing the ladder when he lost his .... and fell.
   A footing   B feet   C standing   D support

8 Some people think that players who consistently behave badly should be .... from the circuit.
   A driven out   B kicked out   C outcast   D outlawed

9 He played far too much competitive sport when he was young; now he is ....
   A burnt away   B burned out   C burnt up   D burned down

10 It would be a good idea to do some scientific .... on the subject.
   A searches   B researching   C researches   D research

11 Nuclear safety is one of the current .... issues.
   A flaming   B burning   C heated   D intense

12 Schools should be run for the .... of the pupils, not the teachers.
   A favour   B interest   C advantage   D benefit

13 The workers made a .... against the management's proposals.
   A stand   B resistance   C fight   D disagreement

14 If you want to persuade the Government to change a law, you can .... a petition.
   A take up   B get up   C sign up   D bring up

15 He sacked one of his employees without a .... of conscience.
   A hint   B sting   C pain   D pang

16 Some .... English teachers have no valid qualifications or experience.
   A so-named   B so-saying   C so-called   D so-mentioned

17 The mentality of people who can shoot animals in cold blood is .... me.
   A unfathomable   B amazing   C past   D beyond

18 He didn't know which candidate to support; he wouldn't .... the fence.
   A come down off   B jump down from   C drop off   D step from

19 He is in prison for the fourth time; he hasn't .... his lesson.
   A learned   B understood   C digested   D taken

20 When asked why he was giving up teaching, he said, "I .... can't face it any more."
   A just   B only   C hardly   D quite

67

21 Someone .... a gun in the classroom.
   A fired   B shot   C burned   D blasted
22 The building was .... on fire accidentally.
   A set   B put   C placed   D made
23 Thieves broke .... last night and stole £500.
   A out   B in   C through   D down
24 He was so fed up with his job that he ....
   A abandoned   B resigned   C re-signed   D dismissed
25 The spokesman for the education authority said that he didn't wish to
   comment ....
   A further   B farther   C more   D longer
26 Long-term unemployment is not .... as a problem by the Government.
   A thought   B considered   C deemed   D regarded
27 Many people have an .... dislike of work.
   A essential   B ingrowing   C inherent   D inherited
28 .... all, most people want health and happiness.
   A Over   B Beyond   C Above   D Through
29 Information concerning the new regulations has been .... distributed
   among the population.
   A largely   B widely   C totally   D lengthily
30 .... parents often produce delinquent children.
   A Permitting   B Allowing   C Permissive   D Tolerable
31 It is wise to approach teaching adolescents with the .... that most of
   them dislike learning and making an effort.
   A pre-condition   B prerequisite   C assumption   D assertion
32 Forcing a student to work .... to resistance.
   A leads   B entails   C produces   D involves
33 The USA .... win the most medals at the next Olympics, but I
   couldn't care less.
   A might really   B could really   C should well   D may well
34 Some teachers think that students work better if left to their own ....
   A means   B devices   C freedom   D options
35 This idea is .... naive as it is wrong.
   A so   B as   C just   D only
36 Teachers are expected to set .... good learning conditions.
   A down   B together   C up   D out
37 Many teachers are .... to vary their methods.
   A incapable   B unable   C unsuited   D unconcerned
38 The achievements of modern science are difficult to ....
   A seize   B grasp   C hold   D catch
39 The composition paper .... a broad range of topics.
   A spreads   B spans   C demonstrates   D crosses
40 His score was so high in the exam that he walked .... a grade A.
   A out with   B out through   C away from   D away with
41 He has a(n) .... appetite for knowledge.
   A thirsty   B unsatisfied   C insatiable   D hungry
42 Private lessons often involve .... teaching.
   A one-by-one   B one-over-one   C one-against-one   D one-to-one
43 People who send their children to private schools have .... time for
   the state educational system.
   A small   B little   C reduced   D never

44 Some parents complain that their children are not being ....
    intellectually at school.
    A pulled   B strained   C forced   D stretched
45 Parents who lack the finances to send their children to a private school have
    to .... the state system.
    A put up with   B support   C stand up to   D put themselves to
46 He was .... of predicting his exam result.
    A careful   B cautious   C prudent   D wary
47 He has built up a solid .... of knowledge in the subject.
    A profoundness   B profundity   C depth   D deepness
48 Researchers are always trying to .... new ground.
    A find   B break   C develop   D penetrate
49 By the age of forty, the adult mind has probably reached the end of its
    creative ....
    A period   B time   C duration   D era
50 It is not always easy at school to .... when a child is especially gifted.
    A learn   B tell   C remark   D disclose

Unit 11

Playing Away

Reading comprehension

The following text has been divided into four sections. Read the sections, and then decide whether the statements which follow are true or false. Be prepared to justify your answers. If you feel that there is not enough evidence to justify true or false, put a question mark.

I later went to Watford with fans of another London club, Chelsea.

5 I travelled with Billy and Neil from Wanstead.

Our journey across London was wary and cautious.

10 Supporters of more than a dozen clubs were on the move and any of them could have made an unprovoked attack. Billy and Neil hid their scarves

15 until they were safely among their own kind.

The trip to Watford was quiet, even though we were packed as tight

20 as sardines into a football excursion train.

"You won't get much trouble beforehand," said Billy. "Nobody

25 wants to get arrested before the match. It's during and after that it happens."

The train was met by a

30 dark blue line of police. Chelsea have a bad reputation for trouble.

"All quiet?" I asked

35 the man collecting the tickets.

"Yeah, nothing much at all," he said with black humour. "We're burying

40 four collectors on Monday."

Outside the station it was no laughing matter. Dog handlers were out in

45 force. We were formed into groups to be marched through the streets to the ground.

I fell in with a group of

50 skinheads, all with nicknames: Bris, Ribs, Chuck and Stapes. They were in their teens and looked threatening, tattoos

55 covering faces and necks.

Ribs, so called because he was so thin, rolled up a trouser leg to show a swastika tattooed on the

60 side of his knee. Other skinheads strolled over proudly to display Nazi "death skull" tattoos.

Their outlandish hair-

65 cuts conceal a secret code.

One "bald" line

through their close-cropped hair means they are members of a gang of at

70 least twenty. Two lines mean they support the National Front, as do red braces and red or white bootlaces.

75 Racial hatred is shown most of all in their treatment of opposition coloured players. When Watford's talented,

80 Jamaican-born striker Luther Blissett ran out he was greeted by chants of "nigger, nigger," and "Sieg Heil" from a sec-

85 tion of the Chelsea fans.

At the back of the stand where thousands of Chelsea fans congregated, a huge Union Jack

90 was unfurled.

Sewn in one corner in white letters a yard high was the Nazi SS symbol.

Streets on the way to

95 the Watford ground were deserted.

I talked to a landlord whose pub was in a state

of siege—just one or two regulars behind locked doors in case of trouble. He didn't want to be named for fear of reprisals.

"I wouldn't dare open up," he said, as line after line of fans glared in through the window, eyes filled with hatred. "It would be more than my life was worth.

"They're absolute animals, some of them. Scum. A disgrace to the human race.

"I've had 'em in here chucking glasses and pies round the place. Smashing windows. When West Ham were here all the chairs disappeared from my forecourt outside. I haven't seen them since.

"Stoke, Chelsea and West Ham are the worst I've seen. There's no reason for the violence. It scares you, it really does."

After going through the turnstiles, the fans were body-searched for weapons. They knew it was going to happen so the haul was tiny—a couple of metal combs and a small penknife.

"Inside the ground it's all fists and boots," a fan told me matter-of-factly.

"You can get weapons through, though. Sharpened 2p pieces for instance. They can do a lot of damage, those, and you can chuck 'em a long way."

Really hard-line groups of fans appoint an "armourer" to look after knives and other weapons. He doesn't go to the match—more than likely he has no interest in football—but keeps the weapons for the trouble afterwards.

In any ground violence is transformed into ritual. The object is to humiliate fans of the other side. They must be out-sung, out-taunted, out-fought.

The prime aim is to capture the opponents' "end"—that part of the ground where most of the home side's fans are massed.

Because policing of the grounds has become more and more successful, such mass pitched battles are rare. At Leeds and Manchester United, for example, the visiting fans I travelled with were put in a separate fenced-in cage, cut off from the home supporters by empty terracing and lines of police.

It's not true that all football hooligans are unintelligent. Many I talked to and who confessed to enjoying trouble, had O and A-Levels and held white-collar jobs.

Most kids seem to grow out of it in their twenties; but by no means all. I saw many men in their thirties and forties among the young fans, chanting and threatening and baiting; dressed in T-shirts, beer-bellies slopping over their waistbands.

Girls, too, can get mixed up in bother. Giggling and goading, they incite the boys to fresh horrors, watching gleefully from the sidelines as a youngster is beaten up or a wall daubed with aerosol hatred: "Arsenal will die." "City kick to kill."

Most of the trouble occurs on the way home after matches.

Sometimes fans run amok in groups, smashing windows and looting.

More often than not the violence springs up suddenly for no apparent reason.

Much of it is cowardly in the extreme. The thugs, in bands of a dozen or so, set on peaceful fans making their way home.

On three separate occasions I saw fans being chased and badly beaten without reason.

One begged for mercy. His reward was a fusillade of kicks in the ribs.

On the train on the way home from the Chelsea game at Watford the obscene songs and drunken bragging started.

A group of eight fans brought carrier bags full of beer on to the train.

After drinking them they opened the window and, swearing, hurled them into the darkness.

A man who had taken his son, aged about eight, to the match, sat in the seat behind them. The little boy, terrified, began to cry.

The father made as if to protest; then thought better of it. He was not a coward. He was a decent man. But he was one against eight and he had his boy to protect.

The little lad sobbed softly as the swearing and can-throwing went on.

His father stared miserably out of the window. *What could he say to his child? How could he possibly explain?*

(From the Sunday Mirror)

Section 1 (lines 1–74)

1 The narrator is one of a gang of football hooligans.
2 Billy and Neil hid their scarves because they didn't want to take risks.
3 Some ticket collectors had already been attacked before the train arrived.
4 The travelling supporters were not allowed into the town centre.
5 Wearing red braces and red or white bootlaces at a football match means you are a Fascist.

Section 2 (lines 75–130)

1 Luther Blissett has extreme right-wing political views.
2 Some football fans seem to identify with Fascist ideology.
3 The owner of the pub closes it completely on match days.
4 The fans who walked past the pub were desperate for a drink.
5 It seems that West Ham supporters are the worst.

Section 3 (lines 131–183)

1 The fans did not anticipate being searched.
2 Some weapons can be concealed from the police.
3 It is unlikely that an 'armourer' follows a particular football team.
4 The hooligans are not interested in football at all.
5 The police are more effective in dealing with hooliganism than before.

Section 4 (lines 184–268)

1 Some hooligans are reasonably well educated.
2 Most hooligans will carry on the violence into middle-age.
3 Females contribute to some of the violence.
4 The victims of the violence are generally innocent fans.
5 The father in the train would have taken action if his son hadn't been with him.

Vocabulary
Explain the meaning of the following words and phrases taken from the passage.

Section 1

1 their own kind (l 16)
2 packed as tight as sardines (ll 19–20)
3 it was no laughing matter (ll 41–42)
4 Dog handlers (l 43)
5 I fell in with (l 48)
6 outlandish (l 63)
7 close-cropped (ll 67–68)
8 braces (l 73)

Section 2

9 striker (l 80)
10 unfurled (l 90)
11 in a state of siege (ll 98–99)
12 regulars (l 100)
13 reprisals (ll 103–104)

14   scum (l 114)
15   chucking (l 117)
16   forecourt (ll 122–123)

Section 3

17   turnstiles (l 132)
18   the fans were body-searched for weapons (ll 132–134)
19   haul (l 136)
20   hard-line groups (ll 149–150)
21   taunted (l 164)
22   pitched battles (ll 174–175)
23   cut off (l 180)

Section 4

24   white collar jobs (l 190)
25   baiting (l 197)
26   beer-bellies (ll 198–199)
27   slopping (l 199)
28   goading (l 203)
29   incite (l 204)
30   gleefully (l 206)
31   daubed (l 209)
32   run amok (ll 215–216)
33   looting (l 218)
34   springs up (l 220)
35   thugs (l 225)
36   set on (l 226)
37   fusillade (ll 233–234)
38   bragging (l 239)
39   made as if to (l 254)
40   sobbed (l 261)

Use of English

A   Fill each of the numbered blanks in the following passage with **one** suitable word.

Football Hooligans

The real troublemakers have turned .... (1) more subtle methods. They try to infiltrate .... (2) opposition end by .... (3) themselves as home fans, chanting the home side's chants and .... (4) the home side's colours. Halfway through the .... (5), at a given signal, they lash .... (6) in all directions, boots and fists flailing, ... (7) a surprise attack.

It is during these .... (8) on enemy territory .... (9) the gang leaders emerge. They win their positions through frightening acts of violence, often against vastly superior numbers, ten or twenty .... (10) one. .... (11) are defeated in the end, usually, pummelled unconscious .... (12) knuckles and toecaps, but they have .... (13) their reputation as hard men. They are dangerous, ... (14) mentally ill, living .... (15) for violence. Even their own followers describe them as 'nutters'.

Why has violence .... (16) such a hold at football matches? I asked this question of scores of fans all .... (17) the country. The sad answer is that kids who have grown up .... (18) the terraces have known nothing .... (19) – they expect violence and, I'm afraid, many .... (20) it.

B Finish each of the following sentences in such a way that it means the same as the sentence printed before it.

EXAMPLE: That table is so heavy that he can't lift it.
That table is too ....
ANSWER: *That table is too heavy for him to lift.*

1 The trip was quiet, even though we were packed as tight as sardines into a football excursion train.
In spite ....

2 They hid their scarves until they were safely among their own kind.
Not until ....

3 Streets on the way to the Watford ground were deserted.
There was ....

4 Stoke, Chelsea and West Ham are the worst I've seen.
I've ....

5 After going through the turnstiles, the fans were body-searched for weapons.
When ....

6 More than likely he has no interest in football.
Football ....

7 Because policing of the grounds has become more successful, such battles are rare.
The reason ....

8 It's not true that all football hooligans are unintelligent.
It would ....

9 His reward was a fusillade of kicks in the ribs.
All ....

10 He was one against eight.
The odds. ....

Oral and written practice

Picture discussion
Look at the photograph and then answer these questions.

1 Describe the scene in the picture.
2 Do you think the injured young man is an innocent victim of violence? Give reasons for your answer.
3 Could you see this sort of incident at a sports event in your country?
4 Why do you think violence of this sort occurs at some football matches?
5 Do you think violence among spectators or players is increasing in other sports? Which ones?

Discussion topic

The following have all been suggested as possible causes of violent spectator behaviour at football matches:

a   Alcohol is on sale in most football stadiums, and freely available elsewhere (even to under-age drinkers).

b   The structure of society: many young people are made to feel worthless in their day-to-day lives (either they have dead-end jobs or they are unemployed); being violent at football matches gives them a kind of importance: they can frighten people.

c   The influence of extreme right-wing political movements on young people (fascist literature is often sold outside football stadiums).

d   A lack of parental control and a general lack of discipline – both at home and at school.

e   Being a member of a crowd tends to obscure an individual's sense of responsibility, and therefore he/she would not generally accept personal responsibility for his/her misdeeds.

f   Violence is a basic human urge, and manifests itself in tribal warfare. Given a general breakdown in law and order and a lack of respect for other people and established conventions, this negative side of man's nature will assert itself.

g   Violent play on the football field leads to violence among the spectators.

The following have all been put forward as possible remedies for the problem of football hooliganism:

a   Football grounds where spectator violence has occurred should be closed for fixed periods.

b   For convicted hooligans, there should be life-bans and stronger prison sentences (even life sentences in extreme cases).

c   Hooligans should be sent to special army units and exposed to severe military-style discipline.

d   Compulsory military service should be restored (at least in Britain, where it does not exist). This would instil discipline and self-control and make young people realise their responsibility to the community.

e   There should be identity cards for all spectators, or a centralised computer pass-system set up. These passes would allow access to any stadium and the codes on them would prevent rival supporters mixing. If you commit an offence, no club would let you into the stadium, or your pass might be taken away from you for a fixed period of time.

f   Closed-circuit TV should be installed in all football grounds, so that troublemakers can be more easily identified.

g   Clubs must improve their stadiums; for example, more seats should be installed, as there seems to be some evidence that people sitting down cause less trouble than those standing up.

h   Rival supporters should be segregated (this is already done in many grounds).

i   The sale of alcohol inside all football grounds should be banned.

j   Football clubs with a consistent record of hooliganism among their fans should be banned from playing in international competitions.

k   Visiting supporters should not be allowed to attend matches, or travel should be made more difficult by removing all cheap trains and coaches.

l   Tougher action against violent play should be taken.

You are going to take part in a popular discussion programme, *Close-up*, on the subject of football hooliganism. You will play one of the people listed below. You will be given enough time to prepare your part. Use some of the ideas above and in the earlier parts of this unit to help you. You might also find it useful to look at the descriptions of some of the other characters in the discussion.

List of characters
Marty Mckee – discussion host

As the host, it is your job to open the discussion, give all your guests an opportunity to express their views, and control the direction of the discussion. Your critics have sometimes accused you of taking sides in order to provoke a heated discussion; however, this sort of programme only holds the interest of the viewers if it is lively and controversial. Look at your list of guests and think of questions you will want to ask them.

Sir Hubert Wilkens – Conservative Member of Parliament and former Army Officer.

You are noted for your strong opinions on such subjects as compulsory military service and law and order. You have recently spoken out on the topic of stiffer penalties for football violence and the possibility of banning football altogether.

Harry Flash – sports journalist

You feel that the problem of football violence has been greatly exaggerated and sensationalised, and that perhaps the media, particularly the popular press, should take a more responsible attitude. You are interested in the development of preventive measures and would like to see the Government, football clubs and all those interested in football, working together to solve the problem.

Manny Read – chairman of a First Division football club and businessman

You have been criticised for knowing very little about football and using your football club as a way of satisfying your own ambitions. You are faced with the problem of wanting to put a stop to the violence which gives football a bad name, but at the same time you must find solutions which are practical, in view of the vast numbers of people attending matches. You would not want people to be discouraged from coming to football matches. As a businessman you must also take into account that the Government receives an enormous tax revenue from football, so should, perhaps, take responsibility for financing any improvements.

Anne Lackey – policewoman

You have frequently been on duty at football matches, and were recently savagely beaten up by a gang of hooligans outside a stadium before a match. As a result of your injuries, you spent two months in hospital. Naturally, you are interested in the role of the police at football matches, especially in what equipment and powers they should be given to help curb violence at these events.

Darren Tebbit – reformed football hooligan

You don't think that most hooligans would be particularly deterred by stronger penalties. You think that the other people in the discussion are missing the point, which is that football hooliganism is more of a social problem. You say that most kids are made to feel insignificant all week: they're ignored at home, they've got boring jobs (if they have a job, that is); but on Saturdays they can be someone important: they can hurt and frighten people!

Ena Poppleton – housewife

You used to live near a football stadium, but were forced to move house because of the constant fighting on the street outside on match days. In a six-month period, you had bricks thrown through your living-room windows five times. You are still undergoing medical treatment for nervous depression.

Written work

1 'Football is the victim of football hooliganism, not the cause of it.' Discuss. (about 350 words)
2 Write an account (about 350 words) of the following incident: You are waiting in a railway station, when two groups of rival football supporters suddenly converge and start fighting. You find yourself caught up in the battle.

Unit 12

Drying Out

Reading Comprehension

You will find after each of the following passages a number of statements, each with four suggested endings. Choose the answer which you think fits best.

First passage

My name is Peter and I'm an alcoholic. With the tremendous help of Alcoholics Anonymous
5 I've been off the booze for just over a year, but being an alcoholic, I take very great care to promise to only abstain for today.
10 (When we swear never never to drink again, it's a sure bet we'll be on the sauce at the very next excuse/provocation.)
15 I want to tell you about seven days and seven nights I spent in a "detox-ification" ward in a big London hospital, because
20 things that I saw and heard there have, I'm afraid, turned me into something of an evangel-ist over the Evil in Our
25 Midst. Don't worry, I'm not going to propose pro-hibition, or claim that alcohol is responsible for 90 per cent of the world's
30 ills. I'm fully aware that millions of people are able to pick up a social drink quite regularly, without finishing up a gibbering
35 wreck in an alcoholic ward.

What does concern me is the increasing amount being spent on booze
40 advertising, the statistics which show that the pub has replaced the coffee bar as a meeting place for young people, and the
45 rather disturbing fact that alcoholism in this coun-try—according to the most august sources—has reached epidemic propor-
50 tions.

I'm not saying stop the advertising, or ban the under-18s from pubs, but I am suggesting that, just
55 as in cigarette advertis-ing, a clear warning should be printed on the bottom of every poster,
every commercial, every
60 bottle and every can. Be-cause those seven days in the thirst cooler shook me so rigid I feel duty bound to offer this warning.
65 First a few mundane facts:

I'm aged 47, a freelance journalist (my name isn't really Peter and none of
70 the names I shall mention are the real names, but this is only for obvious details of anonymity. Ev-ery other detail is true). I
75 began drinking after an unhappy love-affair, and the "pick-up" soon be-came "the holder up." But not for long. Instead
80 of staying upright, I in-creasingly found myself recumbent, without the slightest idea how, or when, I had got there.
85 (One evening I set out for my local and woke up next morning in Reading

station. The rest—as Lewis Carroll put it—"Is a perfect and absolute blank.")

Friends steered me to a doctor, who in turn steered me to a psychiatric unit in a local hospital. I spent a couple of weeks drying out and listening to mild lectures. Upon release, the first thing I did was to head for the nearest pub and celebrate my recovery by getting absolutely paralytic.

A second trip to the same psycho ward merely made me more furtive. I would ask permission to go out to buy some cigarettes and demolish a quarter bottle of vodka (it doesn't smell on the breath) from the handy off-licence three doors away. Once again, I left assuring the doctors that I was a changed man.

The only real change was in my boundless aptitude for assuring myself and every one of my friends and colleagues that "I could hold it" and "no more binges." On the very day I assured my parents that I was in fine shape, I arrived home so drunk that I pushed my fist through the plate glass front door. A friend called an ambulance, and the driver took me to the detoxification unit I mentioned at the beginning of this horror story.

(From *The Guardian*)

1 The writer
   A has not touched alcohol for well over a year.
   B has promised to abstain from drinking for one day.
   C isn't sure whether he'll drink alcohol again or not.
   D believes he won't drink alcohol again.

2 The writer thinks that
   A under-age drinkers should not be allowed in pubs.
   B less should be spent on alcohol advertising.
   C young people should be encouraged to go to coffee bars rather than pubs.
   D the public should be made more aware of the dangers of alcohol.

3 In this story
   A some people's names have been changed.
   B everyone's name has been changed.
   C the people whose names have been changed prefer to remain anonymous
   D all the names and some facts have been changed.

4 The writer began drinking because
   A his girlfriend left him.
   B a personal relationship didn't work out.
   C he needed picking up.
   D he wanted to forget his former girlfriend.

5 After his second period of treatment in the psychiatric unit, the writer
   A was certain he had changed.
   B convinced his friends that he was no longer an alcoholic.
   C was more deceitful.
   D was more sincere.

Second passage

I slept right through the first night and day, and awoke to find myself in a small ward consisting of six beds and not much else, except for four very hungover addicts like myself. Andy was 25 and had been drinking since he was fourteen. He'd been in prison twice for theft (booze money), and was educated and well spoken. Bill was around 45, married, with three children. This was his fifth visit to a detox unit, and he'd been told if he started to drink again he wouldn't last six months.

Harry was 58 and had been drinking steadily since his retirement three years previously. All his money had gone, and he'd been brought in after consuming three bottles of surgical spirit. He was intelligent but in very bad shape both physically and mentally. (He couldn't remember his address, his telephone number, or his son's name.)

Geoff was in his thirties, totally withdrawn, desperately underweight and talked incessantly of being "high" as the only way to live.

The second night I was there, the vacant bed next to mine was abruptly filled by Arthur—a wheezy bronchitic, who spent the whole night being sick and demanding to see his wife. "Your wife doesn't want to see you," the doctor shouted, but Arthur went on asking for his missus till he started to vomit blood at around six o'clock in the morning. By this time he was sober enough to notice the ugly pool of red in the vomit dish and called the doctor because he thought he had a nose bleed. The doctor said very little, felt his stomach and said: "We'll give you something to try and make you stop heaving."

The vomiting continued, about once every three hours, each time more prolonged and more bloody.

Two days later, Arthur died, after a last massive haemorrhage. "Why can't they stop my bloody nose bleeding?" he whispered.

While all this had been going on, bed number six had found an occupant. He was Trevor and was suffering from such violent d.t.'s that he had to be strapped to the bed. ("We're very advanced here," the doctor explained as he did up the strap. "We don't use strait jackets any more.")

Throughout the whole of that night and the next day Trevor screamed and cried and moaned. Occasionally the doctor came in and took his pulse and gave him an injection. It didn't seem to do much good.

"God, leave me alone!" Trevor pleaded, but the hobgoblins he'd invited into his drink-sodden brain wouldn't let him be. "It's after me," Trevor cried, but we were all too shattered to be able to provide much solace.

We all had massive injections of vitamins B and C (alcohol "eats" these essential vitamins (and we were also given strong tranquillisers, but these were tailed off after only four days.

As I sobered up and my tranquillisation was decreased, I began the "hot and colds"—a familiar side-effect experienced by most heavy drinkers as they "come down." One minute your teeth are chattering and your body is covered with goose pimples, the next minute you're lying in a pool of perspiration, with pyjamas and sheets soaking wet. You throw off all your coverings, mopping the sweat that is pouring down your forehead and as you do so, your teeth start chattering and you commence to shiver all over again.

This distressing symptom is accompanied by unsteadiness, nausea, ringing in the ears, a throbbing head and, quite often, double vision. It can last up to three or four months after you have stopped drinking, and I've spoken to alcoholics who still had the morning "hot and colds" a full year after being dry.

(From *The Guardian*)

6   The detoxification ward
    A   eventually had its full quota of patients.
    B   had four people in it.
    C   was never full.
    D   never had more than five people in it.

7   Arthur
    A   thought the doctors should have been able to stop his nose bleeding.
    B   paid no attention to what the doctor said.
    C   was reasonably sober when he was brought in.
    D   was quite sober at six the next morning.

8   Trevor
    A   seemed to be a violent type.
    B   was suffering from hallucinations.
    C   seemed to be in physical pain.
    D   wanted the other patients to comfort him.

9
    A   The injections and tranquillisers were gradually decreased.
    B   The tranquillisers were stopped after four days.
    C   The tranquillisers were found to have no effect after four days.
    D   The tranquillisers were less essential than the injections.

10 'Hot and colds'
    A   are experienced by the majority of heavy drinkers after giving up drinking.
    B   are experienced by some heavy drinkers after giving up drinking.
    C   are an inevitable result of giving up drinking.
    D   can last indefinitely.

Use of English

A   Finish each of the following sentences in such a way that it means the same as the sentence printed before it.

   EXAMPLE: That table is so heavy that he can't lift it.
             That table is too ....
   ANSWER: *That table is too heavy for him to lift*

1   I've been off the booze for over a year.
    I haven't ....

2   What concerns me is the increasing amount being spent on booze advertising.
    The ....

3   The first thing I did was to head for the nearest pub.
    What ....

4   A second trip to the same psycho ward merely made me more furtive.
    The only ....

5   I was so drunk that I pushed by fist through the door.
    I was in ....

6   This was his fifth visit to a detoxification unit.
    He ....

7   He'd been told if he started to drink again he wouldn't last six months.
    They'd told him, '.. '

8   He was intelligent but in very bad shape both physically and mentally.
    Despite ....

9   'Why can't they stop my nose bleeding?' he asked.
    He wanted to ....

10 As I began to sober up, I began the 'hot and colds'.
    No sooner ....

B Fill each of the blanks in the following passage with a suitable phrase.

> EXAMPLE: .... tennis in that heat, you would have been exhausted.
> ANSWER: *If you had played . . .*

A total ban on alcohol – like Prohibition in America in the 1920s and 1930s – is
.... (1) to cure the growing
problem of alcoholism in the Soviet Union, according to Fjodor Uglov, a high-
ranking member of the Academy of Science.

In .... (2) in the Moscow newspaper *Isvestia*, he gives some hair-raising new facts and figures on the problem
and says, 'Unless .... (3)
totally, we will not survive as a nation. There are,' he added, 'forty million
alcoholics in the Soviet Union, and one million die every year. One child in six is
.... (4) some kind of handicap caused by the drinking habits of one ....
.... (5) parents. The problem costs millions of lost pro-
duction hours a year. Industrial accidents caused by drink and resulting in
many .... (6) maimed for life
.... (7) increase. And they are
filling hospital beds urgently needed for other cases.'

But, as with Prohibition days in America, wouldn't a total ban
.... (8) rapid rise in illicit
stills, bootlegging and smuggling? Professor Uglov has ....
.... (9) that too . . . all people convicted of hooch-making,
bootlegging and smuggling..
(10) the death penalty.

Oral and written practice

Picture discussion
Look at the cartoon and answer these questions.

1   Describe what you can see in the cartoon.
2   What is a bottle bank?
3   Who do you think the woman is talking about?
4   Some people say it is wrong to make jokes about conditions like alcoholism.
    What do you think?
5   Is there an alcoholism problem in your country? What causes it and what can
    be done about it?

"He still won't admit he has a drink problem"

Communication activity

You are going to work with another student. You will each be told to look at a communication activity (6 or 9) at the back of the book. Each activity consists of two newspaper stories, one complete and the other with some missing information. By asking your partner questions, fill in the missing information in your incomplete story. Then answer your partner's questions about your other story.

When you both have all the information, decide what changed and what didn't change in George Best's life in the period between the two stories.

Is there anything that seems illogical in the second story?

Do you think his life improved or deteriorated in the period between the two stories?

Written work

1 Write a story entitled:
   'One drink too many'. (about 350 words)
2 The government is likely to introduce controversial new legislation banning the advertising of alcohol on television. Write **two** contrasting statements of position, by:
   a the chairman of a major whisky company.
   b a doctor specialising in alcohol abuse.
   (about 150 words for each)

Unit 13

Smack City

Reading comprehension

Read the following passage, and then decide whether the statements which follow it are true or false. Be prepared to justify your answers. If you feel that there is not enough evidence to justify true or false, put a question mark.

ANY HOPE that the death of a 14-year-old after a 'cocktail' drug overdose will bring sanity to the Liverpool housing estate where he and his school friends bought their 'smack' (heroin) must be slender and remote.

Only the brave or naive would dare predict a change of heart in the teenage culture which supports a heroin habit of alarming proportions or a change in the local realities of life on the 'dole' which make drugs an acceptable opiate to many.

When Jason Fitzsimmons died—still on a life support machine after three days in a coma, the teenage heroin users of the bleak Croxteth estate, Liverpool 11, went about their business as usual.

I was told by one user that very evening: 'I could take you to 12 to 15 people who could sell you heroin, within two minutes' walk of here.'

Croxteth, or 'Crocky,' with its burnt out flats and boarded windows, and its 90 per cent youth unemployment, is the backdrop to last week's tragedy and to the larger problem it has highlighted.

Jason, who lived nearby in Norris Green, was one of scores of heroin users on the estate, most aged 16 to 20 but a few as young as 11 or 12.

A whole generation of young people in the area has been exposed to heroin in a sudden escalation few can explain. 'I left school three years ago,' said a 19-year-old non-user.

'We smoked pot then, and we used to eat magic mushrooms which grew on the playing field, but I don't think I knew anyone on heroin. I hardly knew what it was. Now almost all my pals are using smack.'

The drug hit Croxteth in 1982 and quickly caught on. 'It was a craze, like flower power. Everybody had to try it,' said one youth.

The inquest into Jason's death opens tomorrow but he appears to have succumbed to a mixture of heroin and the heroin substitute, methadone. Police investigating his death are this weekend hoping to talk with the boy's parents.

Even before this tragedy, true-life horror

84

stories were plentiful: school children using their dinner money to buy 'smack', young 90 mothers selling the drug from their babies' prams, pushers' houses barricaded against the police, a 12-year-old boy who dealt 95 in heroin until he gave up using it a few weeks ago.

Croxteth has rich pickings for the media—and the youngsters know it.

100 Two friends of Jason, one who was with him for part of the evening which led to the fatal coma, were torn between grief and 105 asking for cash to pose for a photograph 'smoking' heroin. (Neither has any intention of giving up.)

One, a 16-year-old, 110 claims to have been paid £45 by a Sunday newspaper for his picture.

———

Other youngsters have been given cash by television companies wishing 115 to film the nitty-gritty of drug abuse. Of course, the money has been used to buy drugs—but at least as important as that is the 120 sense this gives of beating the system, of being street-wise and smart.

'Heroin is the most exciting thing that ever happened in Croxteth,' says 125 Mr Allan Parry, a former drug user and now training officer at Mersey regional drug training 130 centre.

He sees Croxteth as a symbol of the political isolation of Liverpool, a testament to what happens when problems are left unsolved. He does 135 not see it as a drug problem, though others would disagree.

In fact, this estate, which now makes headline news as the new 140 'Smack City', is not the worst area of Merseyside. Formerly Birkenhead, and now Bootle, have worse records as heroin 145 trafficking centres. And Croxteth is in better repair than some.

But Croxteth's problems are still prodigious, and the fact that they are 150 part of the general situation in Liverpool only makes them less likely to 155 be solved.

(From the *Observer*)

Section 1 (lines 1–35).

1 Jason Fitzsimmons died as a result of taking a mixture of drugs.
2 Some people in Croxteth probably believe that drugs can help to relieve the stresses and tensions of their everyday lives.
3 Jason died immediately after being taken to hospital.
4 Hard drugs are quite easy to come by in Croxteth.

Section 2 (lines 36–73)

1 There are more than a hundred heroin users on the estate.
2 It is difficult to account for the sudden increase in heroin users in the area.
3 Heroin users were quite common in Croxteth before 1982.
4 Everybody in Croxteth is now a drug addict.

Section 3 (lines 74–112).

1 The authorities know exactly which drugs caused Jason's death.
2 The police know where all the drug pushers live.
3 Some youngsters try to take advantage of the media's interest in the drugs problem.
4 A Sunday newspaper paid money to a 16-year-old for posing for a photograph.

Section 4 (lines 113–158).

1 Allan Parry trains people how to take drugs.
2 He believes that the situation in Croxteth is due more to governmental policies than anything else.

3 Croxteth is the least desirable area in Liverpool.
4 The authorities are doing nothing to change the situation in Croxteth.

Vocabulary
Explain the meaning of the following words and phrases taken from the passage.

Section 1

1 a drug overdose (ll 3–4)
2 slender and remote (ll 9–10)
3 naive (l 11)
4 a change of heart (ll 12–13)
5 on the 'dole' (l 18)
6 an opiate (l 20)
7 a coma (l 25)
8 bleak (l 27)

Section 2

9 burnt out (l 37)
10 boarded (l 38)
11 backdrop (l 41)
12 highlighted (ll 43–44)
13 scores (l 47)
14 a sudden escalation (ll 54–55)
15 the drug hit Croxteth (l 68)
16 caught on (l 70)
17 a craze (l 70)

Section 3

18 inquest (l 74)
19 succumbed to (l 77)
20 true-life (l 85)
21 prams (l 91)
22 pushers (l 92)
23 barricaded (ll 92–93)
24 dealt in (ll 94–95)
25 rich pickings (ll 97–98)
26 torn between (l 104)
27 grief (l 104)

Section 4

28 the nitty-gritty (l 116)
29 beating the system (ll 121–122)
30 street-wise (l 123)
31 smart (l 123)
32 a testament (l 135)
33 heroin trafficking centres (ll 148–149)
34 prodigious (l 153)

Use of English

A Fill each of the numbered blanks in the following passage with **one** suitable word.

Once limited .... (1) several hundred addicts centred in London, heroin use has now become .... (2) common in schoolyards and neighbourhoods .... (3) the country that Prime Minister Margaret Thatcher has .... (4) it threatens to 'undermine a whole generation'.

The publicity campaign has been tailored .... (5) teenagers. But the overall anti-drug offensive is comprehensive, targeted at the sources of the .... (6) and its domestic traffickers as .... (7) as its users.

British officials, who .... (8) the United States as the pacesetter .... (9) in illegal drug use and the fight .... (10) it, have consulted .... (11) with their US counterparts in planning strategy. The government .... (12) begun stationing customs officers in countries that are primary .... (13) of heroin, ... (14) Pakistan, and it is contributing money abroad .... (15) encourage substitution .... (16) poppy crops by others. The maximum .... (17) for trafficking has been changed from 14 years to life .... (18). This autumn, new laws, modelled .... (19) US legislation, will be introduced to loosen banking and privacy regulations to .... (20) investigation and seizure of drug-earned assets.

B For each of the sentences below, write a new sentence as similar as possible in meaning to the original sentence but using the word given in **bold** letters. This word **must not be altered** in any way.

EXAMPLE: It wasn't my intention to frighten you.
mean
ANSWER: *I didn't mean to frighten you.*

1 Any hope that this will change things is slender and remote.
hardly
....

2 Only the brave or naive would dare predict a change of heart.
nobody
....

3 There has been a sudden escalation that few can explain.
inexplicable
....

4 I hardly knew what it was.
idea
....

5 There are schoolchildren using their dinner money to buy 'smack'.
spend
....

6 Neither has any intention of giving up.
both
....

7 A sixteen-year-old claims to have been paid £45.
says
....

8 Heroin is the most exciting thing that has ever happened in Croxteth.
nothing
....

9 He sees Croxteth as a symbol of the political isolation of Liverpool.
symbolises
....

10 Birkenhead has a worse record than Croxteth as a heroin trafficking centre.
bad
....

Oral and written practice

Picture discussion
A Look at the photograph on the next page and answer these questions.

1 This picture has appeared in many newspapers and magazines in Britain. Why do you think this is so?
2 Do you think this picture achieves what it sets out to achieve?
3 Why do you think people start taking drugs?
4 What is the drugs situation in your country?

5 In your country what would happen to someone who was caught by the
   police with drugs in his/her possession?

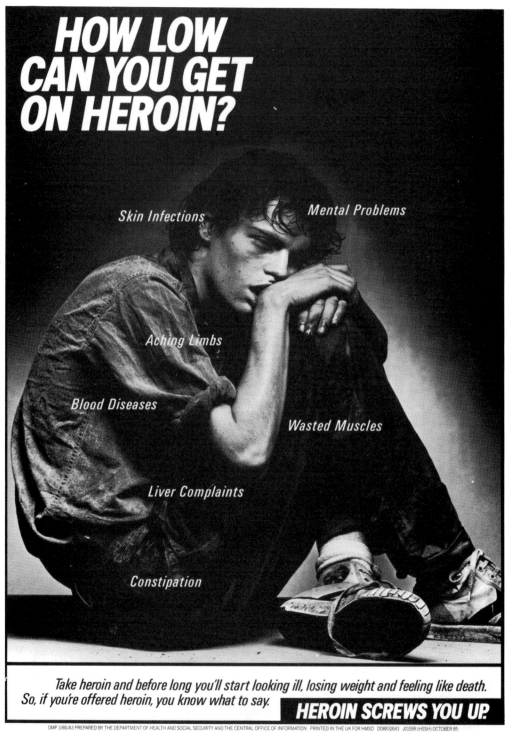

Discussion topic

Decide, in groups, which of the following you think are the most effective ways of fighting drug abuse.

a   Using the media to highlight the problem.

b   Building more drug treatment centres.

c   Motivating parents and communities in general to join the fight against drug abuse.

d   Increasing the resources available to law enforcement, e.g. increasing the penalties for drug trafficking; ensuring that judges pass stiff prison sentences; ensuring that when prison sentences are passed, they are served (i.e. no parole for drug traffickers).

e   Tightening customs controls in countries that are primary drugs sources.

f   A 'maintenance' policy: this tackles demand by providing a legal, controlled supply of the drug. The aim is to take addicts out of the black market.

Written work

1   The five statements below have all been made about the problem of drug abuse. Choose three, and comment on them in three paragraphs of no more than 100 words each.

a   *Having Princess Diana saying 'Don't take drugs' is about as realistic as having Nancy Reagan saying 'Don't take drugs'.*

b   *70% of the crime-wave in some parts of America is drug-based.*

c   *The popular image of a drug addict is someone scrambling around in the gutter who is willing to commit violent crime in order to get his fix. There is so much ignorance about it.*

d   *Many of the brightest people in society, young upwardly mobile professionals, are heavily involved in hard drugs.*

e   *That individuals may take morphine or some other opiate for twenty years or more without showing intellectual or physical deterioration is a common experience of every physician who has studied the subject.*

2   Write a composition (about 350 words) on the following topic: 'Drug abuse is an inevitable problem in present-day society.'

Unit 14

The Finger of Suspicion

Reading comprehension

You will find after the following passage a number of statements, each with four suggested endings. Choose the answer which you think fits best.

Fingerprints, one of the great deciders of innocence or guilt in criminal charges, are now in the dock themselves. This is because of a growing
5 number of claims from defendants that their 'prints' have been 'lifted' and planted at scenes of crimes. And these allegations are being taken seriously by lawyers, judges and policemen because
10 it is possible to move a fingerprint from one spot and place it elsewhere.

With one of the cornerstones of evidence now being placed in doubt a committee of criminal lawyers is car-
15 rying out an inquiry into fingerprinting. The investigation has been ordered by Justice, the prestigious legal organisation, and a report is due early next year. Last night a spokesman for Justice said:
20 "There are an increasing number of cases where people are claiming their prints have been transferred and put on incriminating objects. We are not aiming to establish if these allegations are
25 true or not, but we are questioning current fingerprinting methods as part of a general investigation into scientific evidence. Some of Britain's top criminal lawyers are worried about this increas-
30 ing number of claims."

How can a fingerprint be transferred? A fingermark left on a greasy glass or some other smooth surface can be
'lifted' with a strip of adhesive. It can
35 then be deposited on another, perhaps incriminating, object. Accusations about 'planted prints' were first put up at an Old Bailey IRA bomb trial nine years ago—without success. Fingerprints at
40 the scene of a crime used to be dusted down with fine powder, photographed for identification purposes, then the pictures and the objects carrying the prints were produced in court.

45 However, since 1973 a new method of taking prints has been generally used in Britain. Police experts now use a strip of adhesive tape to 'lift' a print which is then produced in court as evidence.
50 Before 1973 the object on which the prints were found—a bottle, dagger or a gun—used to be shown in court as well. This is no longer necessary. As a result criminals are claiming that their prints
55 have been 'lifted' and planted elsewhere. There have been two successful claims in the United States, though this line of defence has failed in Britain.

According to the ex-chief of Scotland
60 Yard's fingerprint department, Mr Harold Squires, who is now an independent defence witness: "More than 55% of the cases I now get are making these claims. But so far I have not seen any
65 fingerprint evidence that proves the allegations to be true. Petty crooks are

always accusing the police of lifting their prints and planting them at the scene of a crime." According to ex-Chief Super-
70 intendent Squires, lifting a mark and transferring it to another object "requires great skill and trouble". He added: "It's almost impossible but it can be done. It can usually be easily detected
75 by someone like me, but there is a chance that even I may not be able to tell."

Mr Squires sees the new line of defence as an attack on the police by
80 desperate men. He would like the old method of photographing prints and producing them together with the object pictured to be generally used again.

(From the *Daily Express*)

1 Fingerprints have traditionally been regarded as
   A   the only proof of a suspected criminal's innocence or guilt.
   B   one of many proofs of a suspected criminal's innocence or guilt.
   C   no proof of a suspected criminal's innocence or guilt.
   D   a key proof of a suspected criminal's innocence or guilt.

2 The investigation into fingerprinting is
   A   to prove that policemen have been behaving dishonestly.
   B   to establish the truth of the allegations.
   C   part of a wider investigation.
   D   to allay the fears of some top criminal lawyers.

3 The passage suggests that
   A   some of the allegations against fingerprinting are justified.
   B   transferring fingerprints is too much trouble for most policemen.
   C   transferring fingerprints is a very delicate operation.
   D   it is likely that some policemen transfer fingerprints.

4 Since 1973,
   A   fingerprints at the scene of a crime have been dusted down with fine powder and photographed.
   B   it has been necessary to produce in court the objects on which the prints were found
   C   there have been successful claims against police fingerprinting methods in the United States and Great Britain.
   D   police fingerprinting methods have been simplified.

5 Mr Squires seems most concerned about
   A   the number of suspected criminals accusing the police of transferring their fingerprints.
   B   the increasing number of small-time criminals.
   C   the dishonesty of the police.
   D   the unreliability of the new fingerprinting methods.

Vocabulary
A   Find words or phrases in the passage which correspond to the following definitions.

1   people accused in a court of law
2   deliberately placed somewhere (to make someone innocent seem guilty)
3   having a good reputation
4   intending; planning
5   present; of the present time
6   narrow piece of material

7 small knife with a double-edged blade used as a weapon
8 someone who describes what he has seen or heard
9 technical ability; ability to do something well
10 criminals who have no hope of escaping conviction/punishment

B Explain the meaning of the following words and phrases taken from the passage.

1 in the dock (l 3)
2 allegations (l 8)
3 spot (l 11)
4 cornerstones (l 12)
5 evidence (ll 12–13, 28, 49, 65)
6 carrying out (ll 14–15)
7 incriminating (l 23)
8 line of defence (l 58)
9 petty crooks (l 66)
10 detected (l 74)

Use of English

A Finish each of the following sentences in such a way that it means the same as the sentence printed before it.

EXAMPLE: That table is so heavy that he can't lift it.
That table is too ....
ANSWER: *That table is too heavy for him to lift.*

1 It is possible to move a fingerprint from one spot and place it elsewhere
A fingerprint ....

2 A committee of criminal lawyers is carrying out an inquiry into finger-printing.
An inquiry ....

3 A fingerprint can be 'lifted' with a strip of adhesive.
By ....

4 These accusations were first made nine years ago.
It is ....

5 The object on which the prints were found used to be shown.
It used ....

6 There have been two successful claims in the United States, though this line of defence has failed in Britain.
In spite ....

7 There is nothing that proves the allegations to be true.
The truth ....

8 Petty crooks are always accusing the police of lifting their prints.
The police ....

9 Mr Squires sees the new line of defence as an attack on the police by desperate men.
The new line of defence ....

10 He would like the old method to be generally used again.
The method ....

B For each of the sentences below, write a new sentence as similar as possible in meaning to the original sentence, but using the word given in **bold** letters. This word **must not be altered** in any way.

EXAMPLE: It wasn't my intention to frighten you.
mean
ANSWER: *I didn't mean to frighten you.*

1 It is possible to move a fingerprint.
can
....

2 'Justice' is a prestigious legal organisation.
reputation
....

3 A report is due early next year.
come
....

4 We are not aiming to establish if these allegations are true or not.
intention
....

5 Some of Britain's top criminal lawyers are worried about this increasing number of claims.
anxiety
....

6 These accusations were first made nine years ago.
time
....

7 This is no longer legally necessary.
law
....

8 This line of defence has failed in Britain.
success
....

9 Lifting a mark and transferring it requires great skill and trouble.
....
calls
....

10 Mr Squires sees the new line of defence as an attack on the police.
opinion
....

Oral and written practice

Written work
1 'The role of the police is to preserve peace.' Discuss. (about 350 words)
2 You are on holiday with a group of friends in a foreign country and suddenly you are stopped by the police, for no apparent reason, and taken to a police station. Write an account of this incident, and what happened next. (about 350 words)

Picture discussion

Look at the five-part diagram, which demonstrates the process of transferring fingerprints from one place to another. Try to give an explanatory sentence (of not more than ten words) for each part of the diagram. For the first part, an example sentence is already given.

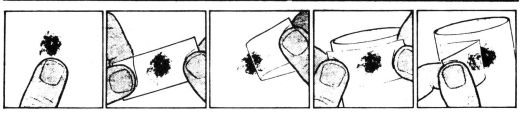

HOW A FINGERPRINT CAN BE TRANSFERRED

THE ORIGINAL PRINT IS LEFT ON THE SIDE OF A TABLE

Answer the following questions:

1. Do you believe that the police would deliberately try to make an innocent person look guilty?
2. Can you think of any other ways of proving someone guilty besides using fingerprints?
3. Have you ever considered a career in the police? Why/why not?
4. What qualities do you think you would need to be a policeman/woman?
5. How has the work of the police changed in the last fifty years?

Discussion topic

How do people feel in general about the police in your particular country? For example:

Do they carry guns? If so, is this regarded as reasonable?

Are they effective in preventing crime?

Are they too hard or soft?

Are they generally polite towards members of the public?

Is there much corruption?

How do you feel about the following statements?

Considering the low intelligence of the average policeman, it's amazing any crimes are solved.

Now, more than ever, you need a bit more under your helmet than a neat haircut. A police officer's job calls for someone with a lot of common sense and a very level head indeed. You can't be over-qualified.

Unit 15

It's a Steal in the City

Reading comprehension

The following text has been broken up into five parts, which have then been mixed up. Decide what the correct sequence should be.

a

'The day I get a man in here stealing because he needs something to eat,' said Mr Miller, 'is the day I'll
5 take him out myself and buy him steak and chips anywhere he wants.'

He picked up a list of the favourite targets. 'Listen.
10 Caviar, tinned salmon, jewellery, fur coats . . . no one actually needs these things. Plain greed I call it.'

Some shoplifters make off
15 with carpets and refrigerators too.

Deep in the heart of the store lies a bank of television consoles from where Mr Mil-
20 ler's men can monitor the comings and goings of everyone in the store, zooming in on tricky sleights of hand and even able to look straight
25 at every till.

b

THERE was such pain and desolation in the small, smoky court reception room last week that you could have
5 easily been forgiven for believing all there were on the next delivery down to hell.

Three women in one cor-
10 ner were wailing discordantly in the manner of an orchestra tuning up. An Arab woman, with her fingers tying her handker-
15 chief into worried knots, had huge tears flopping out of her big, black eyes.

On the other side a pregnant English woman was
20 sitting, fingers interlocked over her bump, blowing with the indignity of it all and, next to her, a small Indian gentleman kept sighing and
25 shaking his head.

In the other corner two Hare Krishna devotees, with pigtails and yellow powdered noses, were chanting man-
30 tras. The floor was covered with squashed cigarette ends. Solicitors drifted in and out in pin-striped serges.

Inside was court Number
35 2 in Great Marlborough Street, London, where a Spanish woman was standing in the dock with her knuckles showing white as
40 her hands gripped the brass rail.

She was, the learned clerk told us, a law student from Barcelona and had been
45 picked up the day before in an Oxford Street store where she had been spotted alternately buying one item and pinching the next. She had
50 taken a total of £88 in goods and had £189 on her. She pleaded guilty and was fined £120 and £40 costs.

c

Next up was an unemployed man from London who had been caught lifting a couple of cassettes and told the magistrate the immortal line: 'I just don't know what came over me.' Each in their turn stepped up with their excuses and tears; each pleaded guilty; each fumbled for words to tell of their sudden weaknesses in the gaudy, glittering palaces of the superstores.

A few of those on shoplifting charges were from London but most were from such cities as New York, New Delhi and Cairo. They were expected, too, since there was a tatty pile of books in the court for the interpreters' oaths—a Church of England Bible, a Jewish Bible, a Catholic Bible, the Koran and the Bhagavad Gita for Hindus.

Another young man stepped into the dock. He was a New York economics student with impeccable credentials whose fingers got carried away in an Oxford Street store.

The magistrate, Mr David Hopkin, seemed slightly baffled by this parade of pointless venality before him. 'Now I am going to ask a question to which I have yet to receive a satisfactory answer,' he said to the student. 'Would you do this in your own country?'

d

As an experience it is about as boring as watching five versions of 'The Borgias' but, from time to time, something does happen which can be video-recorded if necessary. It seems that shoplifters will move goods around for up to an hour before they begin stuffing them into their bags.

Who is going to pinch what next? They don't know, but there is one lovely story of a little old woman in Selfridges who was making for the door when she keeled over with hypothermia. The security staff discovered that she had pinched a frozen chicken and hidden it under her hat. The story was too good to risk asking Mr Miller if there was any truth in it.

e

The young man was given a conditional discharge and next in was a very small, very vexed Indian gentleman who, in a fair imitation of the late Peter Sellers, kept protesting equal amounts of innocence and guilt. He could not understand all the fuss. He wanted to finish all this sorry business now. He meant to pay for the items in the store. He was finally taken away for some legal advice.

The fines seem to mean nothing to most of them. An Egyptian woman was fined £191 that morning for stealing goods to the value of £6.80 and was taking out her purse even as the fines were being spoken. One £7,200 fine on an Arab woman was also paid on the spot.

There are 16 thieving days left to Christmas and one man standing squarely in the blizzard of modern shoplifting—which costs British stores £1,000 million a year—is Mr Michael Miller, the ruddy-faced security chief of Selfridges.

There is, he says, no profile of your average modern shoplifter. Only the other week they picked up an 85-year-old man filching items on his way home from a church meeting but let him go after a stiff warning. They pick up about 40 to 50 a month at Selfridges and prosecute most.

(From the *Observer*)

Vocabulary

Find words or phrases in the text which correspond to the following definitions.

a
1 objects to be stolen (in this context)
2 steal and hurry away
3 observe
4 very skilful, deceptive, manual movements
5 cash-register

b
1 crying
2 falling from
3 expecting a baby
4 humiliation

5 crushed
6 finger-joints
7 held tightly
8 arrested
9 noticed
10 stealing

c
1 stealing
2 spoke hesitantly/uncertainly
3 untidy and shabby-looking
4 a faultless reputation
5 puzzled

d
1 cramming; pushing
2 moving towards
3 collapsed
4 extremely low body temperature
5 take the chance of

e
1 acquittal; release
2 angry; annoyed
3 immediately; right away
4 stealing
5 severe

Use of English

A Fill each of the numbered blanks in the following passage with **one** suitable word.

The girl walked straight .... (1) and looked like she was .... (2) to buy everything in the store. She was very attractive, with blond hair down .... (3) the shoulders of a fawn overcoat. At the back of the big salesroom, way back across rails of fine leather skirts, Maria Armour .... (4) her out. She runs the place which is called 'Jungle', at the corner of Oxford Street and Berwick Street in London.

Maria watched with the same .... (5) of duty often found .... (6) look-outs on ships sailing next to icebergs. The girl smiled over the coats. Then she smoothed her hand on the leather, turned the .... (7) tags on a few and read the figures which .... (8) at £100 and went from there. She knew about quality, and she .... (9) to have class. 'She didn't .... (10) have a carrier bag,' Maria said. 'She was just there with a handbag and wearing an expensive overcoat.'

An empty carrier bag in the hand of .... (11) in Oxford Street is the same as a getaway car. You see someone with an empty carrier bag and they .... (12) as well have 'Thief' tattooed on their forehead.

The girl had now palmed her way through half a wardrobe of designer leather .... (13), taking time to study sizes and cut. She tossed her head at .... (14) and wondered about others. She came nearer to where Maria was. The best lines in 'Jungle' are hung .... (15) that Maria can defend them from the place .... (16) she stands at the till. 'It's hot in here,' the girl seemed to stay. The overcoat came off and was folded .... (17) her arm. Right then, a warning bell went .... (18) inside Maria. There is radar between her and the other sales girls; she didn't .... (19) to say anything to the one called Helena. 'She just knew instinctively that we had a .... (20) in the place,' Maria said.

B This is a continuation of the previous story. This time, fill each of the blanks with a suitable phrase.

What happened next was thrilling. The girl dropped her overcoat, and when it came up all Maria .... (1) sound of an empty hanger swinging on the end of a rail where a £120 .... (2) a second ago. 'It just went in front of my eyes,' Maria said. 'It was there .... (3) wasn't.'

Where it was was inside the overcoat. The girl must .... (4) from a magician. The girl then hurdled through 'Jungle' and reached the pavement in double-quick time. Maria went after her. Maria is 13 stone and looks .... (5) be trouble when it matters. The thief was in Oxford Street turning right when Maria was still going through the shop making up ground. A 73 bus, one of the old kind with an open platform, was moving away slowly from the lights. Everybody downstairs turned around when .... (6) onto the platform hugging the overcoat as if it was a baby.

Maria also hit the platform of the bus. The conductor stopped .... (7) and watched Maria grab the girl with one hand and the rail .... (8) one. She had the girl in an arm lock. The girl was held so tight that her face changed colour. When she stopped struggling, the two of them tumbled off the bus like stuntmen. Now Maria's free hand groped under the overcoat for the leather coat. She put it in a grip the like of which the thief had not experienced before. Out of fright she let .... (9) piece of 'Jungle' property and did not stop to exchange names with Maria.

'She ran off to try some other place, I suppose,' said Maria. But Maria got a terrific look at her face and remembered it. Was this so .... (10) the police a proper description, she was asked. 'Oh, no,' she said. 'It was just so I would recognise her the next time.'

Oral and written practice

Picture discussion
Look at the photograph and then answer these questions.

1 Describe the man in the picture.
2 Why do you think he has a jacket like this?
3 Would you buy anything from him?

4   What would you do if you saw someone shoplifting?
5   Why do you think some wealthy people steal?

Discussion topic

In groups, decide what punishment (or treatment) should be given to these offenders.

a A hotel maid steals a credit card from a guest's bedroom and goes on a spending spree.

b A member of the Royal Family is stopped on the motorway for exceeding the speed limit. It is his/her third such offence in three months.

c A group of Europeans are caught having an illegal drinks party in a Muslim country which observes strict 'no-alcohol' laws.

d A man drives his sick girlfriend to hospital even though he is disqualified from driving. His phone is out of order and the nearest phone boxes have been vandalised.

e A young woman is convicted of using an illegal weapon, a tear-gas spray, after fighting off an attacker late at night.

f A former employee, unfairly dismissed from his job in a supermarket, gets his revenge by setting fire to it one night and causing extensive damage.

g One night, a group of teenage schoolboys return to their school, vandalise some classrooms and steal some money from the secretary's office.

h A senior police officer accepts bribes over a number of years from known criminals.

Now compare your verdicts with other groups.

Written work

1 Write a story entitled 'The Shoplifter'. (about 350 words)
2 'People who are convicted of stealing should be punished on a scale relative to their personal wealth.' Discuss. (about 350 words)

Test 3　Units 11–15　(30 minutes)

Choose the word or phrase which best completes each sentence. Indicate your answer by putting the letter A, B, C or D in the space in each sentence.

1　The hooligans made an .... attack on the other team's supporters.
　　A　unprovoked　B　unprincipled　C　unprotected　D　unpractised
2　In the rush hour, the commuters were packed as .... as sardines in the tube train.
　　A　close　B　firm　C　tight　D　full
3　Finding yourself in the middle of a group of rival fans inside a football stadium is no .... matter.
　　A　smiling　B　laughing　C　reassuring　D　comforting
4　At the political demonstration, the police were .... force.
　　A　out in　B　out with　C　about in　D　about with
5　As he had .... hair and a threatening look, I assumed he was a skinhead.
　　A　close-shaved　B　close-cut　C　close-chopped　D　close-cropped
6　Despite all the efforts of the Race Relations Board, ... hatred seems to be as strong as ever.
　　A　racialism　B　racist　C　racing　D　racial
7　She wanted to remain anonymous for .... of reprisals.
　　A　fear　B　fright　C　worry　D　anxiety
8　The continued use of armies to settle disputes is a .... to the rulers of all nations.
　　A　discredit　B　disgust　C　disrepute　D　disgrace
9　He's a .... male chauvinist: he believes that a woman's place is in the home and that women should not be allowed to vote.
　　A　hard-sell　B　hard-line　C　hard-pressed　D　hard-hit
10　At half-time there was a .... battle between two groups of rival supporters.
　　A　pitched　B　pinched　C　picked　D　pitted
11　They were surrounded by enemy soldiers and therefore cut .... from all possibility of help.
　　A　out　B　away　C　off　D　across
12　He has a white-................. job; he works in a bank.
　　A　collar　B　shirt　C　cap　D　tie
13　His parents hoped he would grow .... his rebellious attitude when he got older.
　　A　out of　B　out from　C　up from　D　up with
14　The frightened people watched from the .... as the hooligans smashed a row of shop windows.
　　A　sidelines　B　sidelights　C　sidewalks　D　sideways
15　In some areas of the city, violence can .... up for no apparent reason.
　　A　jump　B　leap　C　spring　D　shoot
16　He was about to protest, but then .... better of it.
　　A　decided　B　reckoned　C　thought　D　judged
17　Her doctor told her to .... from alcohol.
　　A　cut down　B　restrain　C　abstain　D　hold back
18　In some countries, alcoholism has reached .... proportions.
　　A　academic　B　epidemic　C　endemic　D　epidermic
19　I woke up on the back seat of somebody else's car without the .... idea of how I had got there.
　　A　scarcest　B　smallest　C　scantiest　D　slightest

20 The first thing he did when he arrived in the strange town was to .... for the nearest pub.

A head   B move   C stroll D wander

21 He gets drunk very easily; he can't .... his drink.

A support   B carry   C retain   D hold

22 The drunken patient started to get violent, so the doctor had to have her .... to the bed.

A strapped   B bound   C secured   D attached

23 If you're very cold or frightened, your teeth might start ....

A clapping   B chattering   C clattering   D chatting

24 Accidents involving drunken drivers are .... the increase.

A on   B in   C up   D over

25 The operation will .... a transplant.

A involve   B implicate   C engage   D contain

26 Reformed alcoholics live with the fear of .... back into their old ways.

A slotting   B slinking   C slithering   D slipping

27 The knowledge that the success of the project no longer depended solely on him took a .... off his shoulders.

A responsibility   B heaviness   C handicap   D weight

28 Their next record .... next month.

A brings out   B puts out   C comes out   D shows out

29 A(n) .... is out for his arrest.

A certificate   B warrant   C authorisation   D mandate

30 He died after a drug ....

A overdrive   B overdraft   C overdose   D overdoping

31 Even though its policies have caused massive social deprivation, the Government shows no change of ....

A opinion   B decision   C head   D heart

32 The criminals .... the door against the police.

A barricaded   B blocked   C obstructed   D hindered

33 Since she .... taking drugs, she feels much healthier.

A renounced from   B cut down   C gave up   D cut back

34 The drug problem has been .... news for some time now.

A headtitle   B headline   C headtype   D headlight

35 His health is being .... by drugs and alcohol.

A subverted   B mined   C undermined   D subsided

36 A special committee is carrying .... an inquiry.

A away   B in   C out   D over

37 They are not .... to change the law.

A designing   B aiming   C objecting   D thinking

38 Small-time criminals often .... the police of planting incriminating evidence.

A accuse   B charge   C attack   D criticise

39 No trace of poison was .... in the dead man's blood.

A identified   B exposed   C detected   D disclosed

40 He .... this line of defence as an attack on the police.

A sees   B thinks   C believes   D deduces

41 Before an orchestra plays, the musicians have to tune ....

A in   B on   C out   D up

42 The detective .... her shoplifting.

A spied   B spotted   C recognised   D sighted

43 She .... guilty and was fined.

A admitted   B pleaded   C claimed   D answered

44   When caught with the stolen goods on him, the man said: 'I just don't know what came .... me.'
     A   over   B   on   C   through   D   in
45   He paid the fine on the ....
     A   place   B   spot   C   site   D   instant
46   The thief .... with two overcoats and a jacket.
     A   broke away   B   broke out   C   made off   D   made out
47   Before you try on that jacket, it might be a good idea to look at the price-................. .
     A   label   B   etiquette   C   ticket   D   tag
48   The shoplifter put the stolen goods in a .... bag.
     A   portable   B   handy   C   carrying   D   carrier
49   Some shop assistants know .... when there is a thief on the premises.
     A   instinctively   B   impulsively   C   involuntarily
     D   impressionably
50   As the bus moved away, he just managed to jump onto the ....
     A   stage   B   ramp   C   platform   D   podium

Unit 16

Bosses v. Workers

Reading comprehension

You will find after the following passage a number of statements, each with four suggested endings. Choose the answer which you think fits best.

Henry Clay came from behind him to look at his face, to see whether he was serious or not.

'Don't tell me you agree with them, George?'

'They've no choice, have they? They've been promised a rise for years now, but
5 they're always fobbed off with some lame excuse that the estate can't afford it. It's ridiculous. What's two pound fifty for a day's work these days?'

'But that kind of thing's never been done here before, George.'

'Well it's about time it was then. They'll let you talk until you're blue in the face, but a time comes when you've got to stop talking and show them that you mean business.
10 They'll keep you talking for ever if you let them.'

George Purse was the first gamekeeper to speak out openly on the side of the beaters. Some of the others agreed with him, but not publicly when Henry Clay was there. It was too dangerous. Henry Clay was the Duke's man, and word travelled. Charlie Taylor was the second to speak out.

15 'They'll never get five though, George. Only management get one hundred per cent increases.'

'I know, but if they ask for five they might get four. If they only ask for three they've no room to negotiate, have they?'

'You should have been a union man, George.'
20 'I used to be, didn't I?'

Henry Clay was disgusted with both of them.

'I know what they will get when the Duke gets here. They'll get the bloody sack, all of them. You two an'all if you're not careful.'

He could not understand their attitude. Strikes were not part of his world. He had
25 been born and brought up on the estate. So had his family before him. He had worked all his life on the estate. So had his family before him. Henry Clay's family were loyal servants of the Duke and his family, and Henry felt privileged just to work for them. Even if the Duke did pay him the minimum wage laid down by the National Union of Agricultural Workers (plus an extra five pounds per week for his position as Head
30 keeper). Even if he did work seven days most weeks, and was only allowed the

104

minimum number of holidays laid down by law. And even if it did take an epic of
perseverance and a succession of minor bribes to get repairs done to his house. But
Henry accepted all this exploitation and the subservience which it bred, because he
had been brought up to it. He had been educated from birth to think that paternalism
35 and social inequality were the natural order of things, and therefore immutable.

George Purse and Charlie Taylor did not know how to bring about a social
revolution either. But they did know how to win higher wages. They had been born
in the mining villages which surrounded the estate. They were both from mining
families. Charlie had worked in the pits and George in the steel industry. They had
40 poached the Duke's land before they had become gamekeepers, and now, even
though they were employed by the Duke, their early experiences and loyalties
reasserted themselves. They knew whose side they were on.

And they also knew that if the energy, solidarity and determination to win that
went into industrial confrontations was ever harnessed and used for political ends,
45 then even the Duke would not be immune from the repercussions that would follow
major trade union victories.

(From *The Gamekeeper* by B. Hines)

1   The passage seems to be from
    A   a novel.
    B   a political pamphlet.
    C   a sociology textbook.
    D   an official report on wage differentials.

2   'But that kind of thing's never been done here before' (line 7) means
    A   an increase in pay has never been promised by the Duke before.
    B   the estate workers have never wanted an increase in pay before.
    C   the estate has never been able to afford to give an increase in pay before.
    D   such an increase in pay has never been given on the estate before.

3   Henry Clay was disgusted because
    A   he loved the Duke and his family
    B   he was satisfied with his working conditions.
    C   he felt the workers were already paid enough.
    D   he felt that the Duke's authority over his employees should not be
        challenged.

4   Which of the following statements is correct?
    A   George Purse and Henry Clay had both been born outside the estate.
    B   Henry Clay and Charlie Taylor felt it was a privilege to work on the estate.
    C   Charlie Taylor and George Purse had broken the law before they had been
        employed by the Duke.
    D   Henry Clay and George Purse had both had other jobs before.

5   George Purse and Charlie Taylor felt that
    A   it would be easy to change the status quo.
    B   the Duke and his kind deserved their advantages.
    C   the natural order of things could be challenged.
    D   social inequality was logical.

Vocabulary

A Find words or phrases in the passage which correspond to the following definitions.

1 an increase in pay
2 tricked into accepting something inadequate or valueless
3 give one's opinion plainly and fearlessly
4 decided officially
5 things offered to someone to influence him/her in your favour
6 excessively submissive; willing to assume an inferior status
7 benevolent but oppressive rule
8 that cannot be changed
9 cause to happen
10 coal mines
11 illegally kill or steal animals on someone else's land
12 became strong again; assumed their former importance
13 controlled and used
14 free; secure
15 indirect consequences/effects

B Explain the meaning of the following phrases taken from the passage.

1 lame excuse (l 5)
2 until you're blue in the face (l 8)
3 mean business (l 9)
4 the Duke's man (l 13)
5 word travelled (l 13)
6 no room to negotiate (l 18)
7 get the . . . sack (l 22)
8 an epic of perseverance (ll 31–32)
9 the natural order of things (l 35)
10 for political ends (l 44)

Use of English

A Fill each of the numbered blanks in the following passage with one suitable word.

Years .... (1), a young French girl, Simone Weil, wanting to find .... (2) what work was really .... (3), persuaded a boss to .... (4) her go down a mine and discover what it .... (5) like to use a pneumatic drill .... (6) day. Then she .... (7) a job on the assembly line at the Renault factory. She .... (8) that it was not .... (9) for the miners to take over the .... (10) and car workers to take over the .... (11). They would also have to change the .... (12) technical process to .... (13) the way they wanted to work, and would have to ask: 'Who am I producing this .... (14)? Is it .... (15) producing?'

.... (16) 5,000 workers took over the factory where they had previously been .... (17). .... (18) the carnival of revolution would .... (19) the appeals to .... (20) to work. But what sort of work? Who for? And what for?

B For each of the sentences below, write a new sentence as similar as possible in meaning to the original sentence, but using the word given in **bold** letters. This word **must not be altered** in any way.

EXAMPLE: It wasn't my intention to frighten you.
  mean
ANSWER: *I didn't mean to frighten you.*

1 They've been promised a rise for years now.
  first
  ....

2 The estate can't afford to pay them.
  money
  ....

3 He was the first to speak out openly on the side of the beaters.
  support
  ....

4 Strikes were not part of his world.
  belong ....

5 Henry felt privileged just to work for them.
  privilege
  ....

6 He was paid the minimum wage plus an extra £5 a week for his position as Head Keeper.
  on top
  ....

7 It took a succession of minor bribes to get repairs done.
  another
  ....

8 Paternalism and social inequality were immutable.
  changed
  ....

9 They had poached the Duke's land before they had become gamekeepers.
  prior
  ....

10 Even the Duke would not be immune from the repercussions.
  affect
  ....

Oral and written practice

Written work
Write a composition on one of the following topics:
1 'Job satisfaction is a contradiction in terms.' Discuss. (about 350 words)
2 You are a student doing temporary work in your summer vacation. Unfortunately, one person you are working with is a lot older and obviously resents the fact that you, unlike him/her, are a young person with a bright future. He/she continually tries to provoke you and you find it increasingly difficult not to react, until one day this person plays a nasty trick on you. Describe the incident. (about 350 words)

Picture discussion
Look at the photograph below and answer these questions.

1 What situation do you think is depicted in this photo?
2 Can you see any connection between this photo and any ideas contained in the passage in the first part of this unit?
3 How do you think the police-officers and the workers feel?
4 What events do you think led up to this scene? How might, the situation develop?
5 Do events like this ever occur in your country? If so, give examples. If not, explain why not.

Discussion topic
What do you want in a job? In groups, choose the order of importance of the following points:

1 Good pay
2 Undemanding work
3 Good promotion prospects
4 Job security
5 A chance to use your own ideas
6 A reasonable boss
7 Sociable working hours
8 A chance to learn new skills
9 A chance to be useful to others
10 A chance to have a good social life
11 A staff restaurant on the premises
12 A company car

Now compare your results with the other groups.

Unit 17

Final Placement Syndrome

Reading comprehension

Read the following passage, and then answer the questions which follow it.

Unfortunately, the medical profession has so far failed to recognize the existence of the Final Placement Syndrome! In fact, that profession has
5 displayed a frigid hostility toward my application of hierarchiology to the pseudo-science of diagnostics. However, truth will out! Time and the increasingly tumultuous social order
10 inevitably will bring enlightenment.

Three Medical Errors (a)

Final Placement Syndrome patients often rationalize the situation: they claim that their occupational incompe-
15 tence is the result of their physical ailments. "If only I could get rid of these headaches, I could concentrate on my work."

Or "If only I could get my digestion
20 fixed up . . ."

Or "If I could kick the booze . . ."

Or "If I could get just one good night's sleep . . ."

Some medical men, my survey re-
25 veals, accept this rationalization at face value, and attack the physical symptoms without any search for their cause.

This attack is made by medication or
30 surgery, either of which may give temporary, *but only temporary, relief.* The patient cannot be drugged into competence and there is no tumor of incompetence which can be removed
35 by a stroke of the scalpel. *Good advice* is equally ineffective.

"Take it easy."
"Don't work so hard."
"Learn to relax."
40 Such soothing suggestions are useless. Many F.P.S. patients feel anxious because they know quite well that they are doing very little useful work. They are unlikely to follow any suggestion
45 that they should do still less.

Another futile approach is that of *the friendly philosopher:*
"Stop trying to solve all the world's problems."
50 "Everybody has troubles. You're no worse off than lots of other people."
"You have to expect some of these problems at your age."

Few F.P.S. patients are susceptible
55 to such cracker-barrel wisdom. Most of them are quite self-centred: they show little interest in philosophy or in other people's problems. They are only trying to solve the problems of
60 their jobs.

Threats are often employed:
"If you carry on like this, you will end up in hospital."
"Unless you slow down, you're
65 going to have a really serious attack."

This is futile. The patient cannot help but "carry on like this." The only thing that would change his way of life would be a promotion, and he will not
70 get that, because he has reached his level.

Another much-used line of advice is the *exhortation to self-denial.*

"Go on a diet."
75 "Cut down on your drinking."
"Stop smoking."
"Give up night life."
"Curb your sex life."
This is usually ineffective. The
80 F.P.S. patient is already depressed
because he can take no pleasure in his
work. Why should he give up the few
pleasures he has outside of work?
Moreover, many men feel that there
85 is a certain aura of competence associated with heavy indulgence in bodily
pleasures. It is reflected in such
phrases as "He has a *wonderful* appetite," "He's a *great* ladies' man," and
90 "He can hold his liquor." Such praise
is doubly sweet to the man who has
little else to be praised for; he will be
reluctant to give it up.

Three Medical Errors (b)

95 A second group of physicians,
finding nothing organically wrong with
an F.P.S. patient, will try to persuade
him that *his symptoms do not exist!*
"There's really nothing wrong with
100 you. Just take these tranquillizers."
"Get your mind off yourself. These
symptoms are only imaginary. It's your
nerves."
Such advice, of course, produces no
105 lasting improvement. The patient

knows that he is suffering, whether the
physician will admit it or not.
A common result is that the patient
loses faith in the physician, and runs to
110 another one, seeking someone who
"understands his case" better. He may
lose faith altogether in orthodox medicine and start consulting pseudo-
medical practitioners.

115 *Three Medical Errors (c)*

After medication and surgery have
failed, psychotherapy is sometimes
tried. It seldom succeeds, because it
can have no effect on the root cause of
120 the F.P.S., which is the patient's voca-
tional incompetence.

A Smattering of Sense

The only treatment, my survey
shows, which gives any relief for the
125 F.P.S. is distraction therapy.
"Learn to play bridge."
"Start a stamp collection."
"Take up gardening."
"Learn barbecue cookery."
130 "Paint pictures by numbers."
Typically, the doctor senses the
patient's copelessness with regard to
his job, and so tries to divert his
attention to something that he can
135 cope with.

(From *The Peter Principle* by Dr L J Peter and R Hull)

1 What do you understand by 'the increasingly tumultuous social order' (line 9)?
2 According to the writer, which two things are basically wrong with the medical approach to the problem?
3 What would 'a stroke of the scalpel' (line 35) be?
4 Why does the writer believe that the philosophical approach is useless?
5 What does 'them' (line 56) refer to?
6 What does 'he has reached his level' (lines 70–71) mean?
7 Why would the advice contained in lines 74–78 not have the desired effect?
8 Why do some doctors try to persuade the patient that there is nothing wrong with him?
9 Why is 'understands his case' (line 111) in inverted commas?
10 What do you understand by 'pseudo-medical practitioners' (lines 113–114)?
11 What is meant by 'copelessness' (line 132) and 'something that he can cope with' (lines 134–135)?
12 In 100–120 words, summarise the medical advice given to Final Placement Syndrome patients.

Use of English

A Fill each of the numbered blanks in the following passage with **one** suitable word.

'Networking' is the new buzzword .... (1) the under thirties, so much so that I recently heard a senior corporate officer .... (2) to have it explained to him.

Networking isn't new, or a Yuppie invention. For those over thirty (hands up, please!), it simply boils .... (3) to doing favours for your friends – or, if you like, to the old .... (4), 'It's not who you are, it's who you know.' The key .... (5) networking is mutual support, not friendship as such. Some of the people you network with may .... (6) friends or become friends, some not. It doesn't matter. Members of a network are there to .... (7) their own careers by helping each .... (8).

This form of the 'buddy system' is as old as mankind. Primitive people formed networks because they knew that sooner or later their .... (9) survival would depend .... (10) the willingness of others to help. The same is true in most rural societies, including our own, today. .... (11) your neighbours don't come to help out when there's a problem, you're in trouble, and they won't come for you if you don't come for them. If this seems like a revolutionary .... (12) to young people today, it's because we've become an urban nation in .... (13) our neighbours are mostly strangers, many of them hostile. In a society where everybody lives behind .... (14) doors and minds his or her own .... (15), the idea of a social contract seems unfamiliar.

For .... (16) entering the corporate world, the importance of networking .... (17) be overestimated. However, there are certain rules that have to be followed. First of all, you have to .... (18) in mind that a successful network within a corporation cannot be based .... (19) people who are in the same department as you, or who do the same kind of job. Your direct .... (20) make poor networkers, since you're all pursuing the same goal. You can't expect a fellow networker to help you get the job he or she also wants. Human nature doesn't extend that far.

B For each of the sentences below, write a new sentence as similar as possible in meaning to the original sentence, but using the word given in **bold** letters. This word **must not be altered** in any way.

EXAMPLE: It wasn't my intention to frighten you.
          mean
ANSWER: *I didn't mean to frighten you.*

1 The medical profession has failed to recognize the existence of the Final Placement Syndrome.
   exists
   ....

2 They claim that their occupational incompetence is the result of their physical ailments.
   cause
   ....

3   You're no worse off than lots of other people.
    position

    ....

4   They show little interest in philosophy.
    much

    ....

5   Go on a diet.
    down

    ....

6   This advice is usually ineffective.
    work

    ....

7   He will be reluctant to give it up.
    feel

    ....

8   These symptoms are only imaginary.
    figment

    ....

9   He may lose faith altogether in orthodox medicine.
    chance

    ....

10 Start a stamp collection.
    take

    ....

Oral and written practice

Picture discussion
Look at the two photographs and answer these questions.

1   Describe the two photographs.
2   Which of the two photographs, in your opinion, might be said to illustrate
    Final Placement Syndrome?
3   Where would you expect to find two photographs together like this?
4   In your experience, would you say that most people in a working
    environment are more like the man on the left or the man on the right? Why?
5   If you were a boss, and you happened to bump into the man on the right (one
    of your employees), how would you react?

Communication activity

In pairs, look at the following list of jobs and try to decide what type of jobs they are. When you are ready, turn to one of the communication activities (3 or 11) at the back of the book and read the advertisements for each job to see if they give you a clear idea. Discuss your findings with your partner.

The jobs are:

Butler   Athletics Motivator
Fieldworker   Racial Harassment Worker
Retail Depot Clerk   Alcohol Project Worker
Housekeeper/Life Skills Teacher   Acqua Maid

Written work

1 Choose one of the jobs from the list on page 113 and write the letter of application. (about 200 words)

2 The following statements have all been made about work. Choose three and comment on them in not more than 100 words each:

a *Work to me is a void, and I begrudge every precious minute of my time that it takes. I only go to work because I have no choice.* (factory worker)

b *I come to work to grind people's noses into the dust.* (employer)

c *Every time I'm asked to write the label for a can of beans, I feel absurd. And every time my cheque arrives, I'm glad I'm not earning as little as the girl who worked the machine that put the beans in the tin.* (advertising copy writer)

d *To wake in the morning with a fear of the day ahead, to force a hasty breakfast down an unwilling throat, and then set off for work with pounding heart and frozen face had become habitual, and I had turned to tranquillisers to help me along.* (secondary school teacher)

e *Work is what gives human beings their self-respect and the respect of others, and is the deepest source of achievement and satisfaction in life.* (politician)

f *I believe in the dignity of labour.* (politician)
   That's because you've never done any. (a member of his constituency)

Unit 18

A Neutered Society

Reading comprehension

Read the following two passages, and then decide whether the statements which follow are true or false. Be prepared to justify your answers. If you feel that there is not enough evidence to justify true or false, put a question mark.

First passage

Will those small boys ever get over it?

I become amazed pretty easily these days—particularly when I read the nonsense notions prop-
5 ounded by some departments of the Inner London Education Authority. It seems that certain of them are campaigning
10 for a "role reversal" in primary schools—"to root out sexual bias in toddler thinking and remove any sexist images".

15 Well that's what I read. To this end it appears that, as a pioneer scheme, it is suggested that boys in the nursery class at one
20 primary school are to be taught to cook and the girls are to be given engineering sets. Not bad thinking at all. I'm all for
25 encouraging small children to be handy about the house—if only the scheme stopped there. "While the girls will be
30 allowed to play football, the boys, dressed in skirts and petticoats and carrying handbags, will potter in the Wendy House."
35 Can you beat that for daftness? How crazy and mixed up can any "educa-
tion" authority get?

I am reminded of the
40 time when, years ago, my godson took the lead as a "mole" in a school pantomime. For some weeks he behaved precisely like a
45 mole. He scrabbled with his food as if with blunt paws, he squinted with his eyes half open and insisted on sleeping
50 under his bed "like in a hole". It was quite a while before we could persuade him to romp around the garden in the early spring
55 sunshine. Had he been

115

encouraged at school to wear skirts and petticoats and carry a handbag, it might have taken still lon-60 ger for him to get used to being a five-year-old-boy. Goodness knows he might, these days, be bounding round town in 65 drag. Only happily, and maybe not surprisingly, he's mining in Australia. I do hope he did not go mining because he related 70 to his early kindergarten life as a make-believe mole in a fantasy hole!

(From the Sunday Express)

1 Some educationalists believe that there may be sexual prejudice among small children.
2 The writer is against the whole scheme.
3 The 'role reversal' scheme will be tried out in most London primary schools.
4 The writer's godson developed a fear of sunshine.
5 The writer believes that if her godson had been exposed to a 'role reversal' system of education, he would have become effeminate.
6 The writer is not sure whether her godson's acting the part of a mole in his childhood had any bearing on his decision to go mining.

Second passage

'A book I've been reading explains the difference between men and women. It explains,' he went on, 'why women don't do any of the things that they complain that only men are allowed to do. When this one', he indicated the baby in his arms, 'was in the womb it was subjected to one chemical, but if
5 it had been a boy it would have been subjected to another. It's the chemical structure of the brain that makes a boy behave one way and a girl another. This same chemical structure is the basis of masculine assertiveness. With a girl it has the opposite effect, and even though they might be like my daughter, who's an absolute cow, it's not the kind of assertiveness that creates
10 new religions, great paintings or new technologies. It's a resigned aggression which accommodates the world as it is rather than instinctively seeking to change it.'
He raised the baby to his shoulder, winded it, lowered it and, wiping milk from the corner of its mouth, added, 'All these women trying to do what men
15 do are not only wasting their time but also forfeiting their intrinsic nature, distorting and perverting it for good.'
The baby slept, its head propped on his arm.
'I should have changed its nappy,' he said. 'I'll have to leave it now. I don't want to wake it again.'
20 He stood, adjusted the baby against his arm and, the bottle in his hand, tip-toed to the door. 'All this,' he went on, 'is the latest fashion. When women have given up capering around like men and are reconciled to a world of male assertiveness, they'll go back to what they were before. All this upsurge,' he continued, 'will have been for nothing.'

(From Present Times by D. Storey)

7 The speaker thinks that women are inferior to men.
8 He says that the differences between men and women are predetermined.
9 Apparently, it is not unusual for women to be aggressive.
10 The speaker thinks his daughter is ugly.
11 He feels that women will have to become more aggressive if they want to change the world.
12 According to him, the feminist movement is just a passing trend.

Vocabulary

A Explain the meaning of the following words and phrases taken from the first passage.

1 propounded (ll 4–5)
2 campaigning (l 9)
3 root out (l 12)
4 bias (l 12)
5 toddler (l 13)
6 pioneer scheme (l 17)
7 I'm all for (l 24)
8 handy (l 26)
9 potter (l 34)
10 Can you beat that for daftness? (ll 35–36)
11 mixed up (l 37)
12 took the lead (l 41)
13 pantomime (ll 42–43)
14 scrabbled (l 45)
15 blunt (l 46)
16 paws (l 47)
17 squinted (l 47)
18 romp around (l 53)
19 bounding (l 64)
20 in drag (ll 64–65)

B Find words or phrases in the second passage which correspond to the following definitions.

1 organ in a woman in which a child develops
2 exposed
3 self-assurance; aggressive behaviour
4 trying
5 giving up; renouncing
6 innate; inherent; genuine
7 changing (something) in an unnatural or a wrong way
8 supported
9 behaving foolishly/irresponsibly
10 revolt; rebellion

Use of English

A Fill each of the numbered blanks in the following passage with **one** suitable word.

When cultural differences, even within the same city, are so wide, it is hardly .... (1) to maintain that there is a 'normal' degree of aggression which .... (2) men or women could be expected to display. Yet the biological difference remains; and, when we come to study the relations between men and women within .... (3) particular cultural setting we find that for the male to be relatively more dominant and the female relatively .... (4) so makes both for stability of the family and also for sexual happiness between the couple.

The words and phrases we commonly employ .... (5) describing intellectual activity are aggressive in tone. In mastering intellectual problems, attacking difficulties, sharpening their wits, or penetrating

.... (6) the heart of a mystery, men are using, however peaceably, energy .... (7), in the last analysis, is derived from the primitive aggressive drive to .... (8) ascendancy over the environment. And it is highly probable that the undoubted .... (9) of the male sex in intellectual and creative achievement is related to their .... (10) endowment of aggression. It is true that women have often been badly .... (11) by men, deprived .... (12) opportunities of education, denigrated, or forced to be unnecessarily subservient. But, even when women have been given the .... (13) to cultivate the arts and sciences, remarkably .... (14) have produced original work of outstanding quality, and there have been no women of genius comparable to Michelangelo, Beethoven or Goethe. The hypothesis that women, if .... (15) given the opportunity and encouragement, would .... (16) or surpass the creative achievements of men is hardly defensible. It is a sad reflection upon our civilisation that we .... (17) even be concerned with such a problem, for its existence demonstrates our alienation from our own instinctive roots.

Women have no .... (18) to compete with men; for what they alone can do is the more essential. Love, the bearing of children and the making of a home are creative .... (19) without which we should perish; and only a civilisation in .... (20) basic values have become distorted would make these sterile comparisons.

B Finish each of the following sentences in such a way that it means the same as the sentence printed before it.

    EXAMPLE: That table is so heavy that he can't lift it.
                That table is too ....
    ANSWER: *That table is too heavy for him to lift.*

1 It seems that some of them are campaigning for 'role reversal'.
    Some of them ....

2 I'm all for that idea.
    I've got ....

3 Can you beat that for daftness?
    Have you ....

4 It was quite a while before we could persuade him to play in the garden.
    It took ....

5 I hope that he did not go mining because he related to his early kindergarten life.
    I hope that relating ....

6 A book I've been reading explains the difference between men and women.
    The difference ....

7 If it had been a boy, it would have been subjected to another chemical.
    Had ....

8 Even though they might be like my daughter, it's not a creative kind of assertiveness.
    Despite ....

9 All these women are not only wasting their time but forfeiting their intrinsic nature.
Not only ....

10 I should have changed its nappy.
It's a pity ....

Oral and written practice

Picture discussion
Look at the photograph below and answer the questions which follow.

1 What is your reaction to this photograph?
2 Do you think it is 'normal' for a woman to look like this?
3 Would this fall into the category of 'role reversal' mentioned at the beginning of this unit? Why/why not?
4 Do you think that a woman who goes in for body-building changes mentally as well as physically? If so, how?
5 Can you think of any other so-called minority sports or leisure activities which have gained in popularity in recent years? Why have they become more popular?

Discussion topic

The following five passages have been taken from feminist literature. Read through them and decide in groups whether you find the ideas expressed in them reasonable or unreasonable. Give your reasons.

As a result of a court decision, former Miss Ellen Cooperman can now legally call herself Ms Ellen Cooperperson. A member of the National Organisation for Women, it took three years of campaigning for Ms Cooperperson to achieve her objective.

Women in dire straits should be given special legal status allowing them to steal food and clothing and cheat on welfare to provide for themselves and their families, says a report by a group of feminist legal experts.

Observe any school playground: the physical space carved out by the vigorous activities of young males literally pushes young females to the edges. Football takes up much more room than skipping. The securing of territory and the retention of it by physical/verbal means is a recurrent symbol and expression of male dominance and female subordination.

HAVE YOU EVER WANTED TO TRY OPERATING A FORK LIFT TRUCK?

If you are a woman, here is your chance.
To mark International Women's Day on March 8
The GLC is organising a week of events which include the opportunity to use heavy machinery at open days for women at GLC refuse depots.

Four girls aged 16 to 18 turned to mugging because "all the boys at college did it and they thought why not the girls", it was stated at Inner London Crown Court yesterday. They hatched the plot during a typing lesson.

Written work

Men get the needle

SEX equality campaigner Gerry Popplestone wants male commuters to change their macho image—by knitting on the train.

Gerry, who lectures in men's emotions at a London college, says public knitting could help smash male domination of society and improve the lot of women.

He is taking a leading role in the battle but said: "Unfortunately most men look away, embarrassed, when I bring out my knitting needles on the train.

"But a minority will talk about what I am doing."

1 Imagine that Gerry Popplestone sits down opposite you, produces his knitting and, noticing that you are staring at him disbelievingly, says: "You don't mind, do you?" Write the rest of the conversation in dialogue form. (about 350 words)

2 You spot the following job advertisement in a newspaper. You are appalled by what you consider to be its sexist prejudice. Write a letter to the personnel manager concerned, giving your reasons and threatening legal action. (about 200 words)

HELP—URGENT
Smiling, Efficient Secretary
needed for top company

The suitable candidate will have:
—fluent English and French
—a minimum of 3 years' experience
—excellent typing skills

She should also:
be slim and good-looking, of smart appearance, no more than 30 years old, have a good sense of humour and, above all, be free of 'personal problems'.

Interested? For more information, call 01-380 1955.

Unit 19

Men on the Receiving End

Reading comprehension

The following text has been broken up into five parts, which have then been mixed up. Decide what the correct sequence should be.

a

However, women have to be quick, and must steel themselves to see the thing through. "The idea 5 is not to hit and run away, the idea is to get him on the ground injured enough to stay there till the police come." Is this 10 an idle dream? Mr Biffen says not.

"I get furious," he says, "when psychologists say women who resist 15 get killed—how many of them have learned how to fight? Nobody would tell a man not to learn karate because he'd get beaten 20 up. If women could release themselves from men's physical dominance, they'd realise the truth, that they're 25 equal."

He has a waiting list for his classes. He tells his pupils: "Regard it as a competition of minds. 30 Don't ever give up, even if you come round and he's on top of you. Believe me, I used to do boxing and when I won, 35 the bruises didn't hurt."

He is also confident. There is no charge to anyone who decides after the first session that his 40 philosophy in practice is not for them.

About 20 women attend his weekly evening classes. They can wear 45 high heels and tight clothes—the Biffen method is supposed to work whatever your taste in clothes. Some bring 50 boyfriends and husbands to use as specimen attackers. Women are reluctant to hit each other hard enough, they say.

b

How many of us, for instance, know that to clap both hands at the same time against both of 5 an attacker's ears can burst the ear-drums and possibly cause fatal injury? Or how many know that it takes as little as 8lb 10 of pressure to break an elbow (that's the strength it takes to hold two bags of sugar in an outstretched arm) and 5lb of press- 15 ure to bust a wrist?

Sometimes an attacker's hold which seems the most secure and looks 20 dramatic is one of the easiest to break. If you are grabbed from behind with both the assailant's arms around your body, you can keep your arms 25 straight down by your sides, then work your hands round to his groin.

Or, if held by the shoulders, it's possible to escape by pivoting from the waist, swinging an arm up and back in an arc, and bending the other arm at the elbow. The elbow should be used simultaneously to slug him on the temples. It is, in fact, much simpler to do than to describe and should be enough to knock him out if done accurately.

Years of conditioning may have made women something of an easy touch when it comes to violence by men, but Chris Biffen refuses to accept that state of affairs. Over the years, he says, women have done heavy duty work, in the fields and the factories, and they cope with the fine precise work of the doctor, architect, lawyer, or lacemaker. As he says, it is a mite strange to think that we are incapable of coordinating hand and eye long enough to deliver a good punch. He certainly hopes that more women will take the point and get in trim—the only people who stand to lose, after all, are the bully boys.

c

There is a bit of a warm up. The women watch and copy, something which, at moments, looks like a cross between modern dance and slapstick. Chris Biffen uses two large fellow instructors, with whom he demonstrates the four ways to prevent yourself being strangled; how to break the elbow of anyone who grabs you by the hair; how to break the wrist of someone who grabs you by the arm; how to cause an assailant to bite out his own tongue.

To get it right you need to operate at reflex speed, but it is a fascinating beginning. As arms twist, and legs trip and bodies fall with a thud, Mr Biffen makes it all the more memorable with a wry commentary.

"I'm going to use a real knife because no one is going to attack you with a rubber one . . . look at the gun and if it says Mickey Mouse Club on the side, forget about it . . . if he's got hold of your hair, place your hand on top of his and anchor it there, don't try and pull his hand off, you'll end up free but bald . . ."

The women appeared to be at different stages in the ten lesson course. Some looked frail and their death-dealing blows very flimsy. Their "attackers" looked touchingly benign. Others seemed able, as Mr Biffen would say, to "look after themselves".

d

WHY knuckle under to male violence when you can tear off his ear? After all, it takes only the same strength as folding the Guardian in half and tearing off the corner. In fact, if grabbed from behind by some nasty brute you can release yourself from his grip and knock him unconscious in one go—if you know the move.

So promises Chris Biffen, a delicately-built teacher of the martial arts who is an expert in six different Japanese ways of killing people with his bare hands. He has devised what he claims is a unique system of self defence for women.

There is, he says, no attacker's grasp that cannot be countered, and he challenges any woman to bring the largest, heaviest, toughest man she can find to his class, so he can demonstrate the invincible principles of Ju-te-do—"the way of gentle hands".

Mr Biffen believes that women can fight as expertly and effectively as men. If trained to use methods that suit them, physically and psychologically, women have advantages over men, he says, in spite of their different build. A lower centre of gravity, lower height and more symmetrical shape should give them better balance and stability. Women, though not conditioned to be physically agressive, can turn the assailant's strength back on him by appearing to yield. You don't need bulk if you can use your limbs as levers. "A cunning hand needs less strength," he says. "Fight dirty."

e

Mrs Sharon Piere, aged 25, on her tenth lesson, threw to the ground a man twice her weight, and demonstrated how to escape the grip of two men at once by delivering to both of them a sock in the jaw or the temple.

"I keep reminding myself that I'm not going to be attacked in a nice hall with mats on the floor. This is lovely, but could I do it in an alley?" she says.

She said she felt more confident for having learned self defence. "At least you know you won't panic. He's thrown so much at you. Even if the technique doesn't stick in your mind, once you realise what you are capable of you'd be so angry that anyone dared to touch you."

The Biffen method is based on simple principles. Always go towards the thumb when someone is gripping you; swing from the waist and hip when you punch. Some ideas seem so obvious it is surprising most women are quite unaware of them.

(From *The Guardian*)

Vocabulary

Explain the meaning of the following words and phrases taken from the text.

a
1 steel themselves (l 3)
2 see the thing through (ll 3–4)
3 an idle dream (l 10)
4 get beaten up (ll 19–20)
5 come round (l 31)
6 bruises (l 35)
7 is not for them (ll 40–41)
8 high heels (l 45)
9 specimen attackers (ll 51–52)
10 reluctant (l 52)

b
1 clap (l 3)
2 outstretched (ll 13–14)
3 bust (l 15)
4 assailant (l 22)
5 work . . . round (ll 26–27)
6 pivoting (l 30)
7 slug (l 36)
8 an easy touch (ll 45–46)
9 get in trim (l 65)
10 bully boys (ll 67–68)

c
1 warm up (ll 1–2)
2 cross between (l 5)
3 slapstick (l 6)
4 trip (l 24)
5 thud (l 25)
6 wry (l 27)
7 anchor (l 39)
8 frail (l 46)
9 flimsy (l 48)
10 benign (l 50)

d
1 knuckle under to (l 1)
2 tear off (l 3)
3 countered (l 26)
4 invincible (l 32)
5 turn . . . back on him (ll 52–53)
6 yield (l 54)
7 bulk (l 55)
8 levers (l 56)
9 cunning (l 57)
10 Fight dirty (l 59)

e
1 sock (l 8)
2 jaw (l 9)
3 alley (l 15)
4 doesn't stick in your mind (ll 23–24)
5 punch (l 35)

Use of English

A Finish each of the following sentences in such a way that it means the same as the sentence printed before it.

EXAMPLE: That table is so heavy that he can't lift it.
                 That table is too ....

ANSWER: *That table is too heavy for him to lift.*

1 How many of them have learned how to fight?
I'd like ....

2 Women are reluctant to hit each other hard enough.
Women don't ....

3 It takes as little as 8lbs of pressure to break an elbow.
8lbs of pressure ....

4 It is much simpler to do than to describe.
Describing ....

5 Years of conditioning may have made women something of an easy touch.
Women ....

6 You'll end up free but bald.
In spite ....

7 It is a unique system of self-defence for women.
There is ....

8 Women have advantages over men in spite of their different build.
Though ....

9 She said she felt more confident now that she had learned self-defence.
'I ....

10 The Biffen method is based on simple principles.
Simple principles ....

B For each of the sentences below, write a new sentence as similar as possible in meaning to the original sentence, but using the word given in **bold** letters. This word **must not be altered** in any way.

EXAMPLE: It wasn't my intention to frighten you.
           mean

ANSWER: *I didn't mean to frighten you.*

1 Regard it as a competition of minds.
look
....

2 When I won, the bruises didn't hurt.
feel
....

3 The Biffen method is supposed to work whatever your taste in clothes.
however
....

4 He hopes more women will get in trim.
like
....

5   Biffen makes it more memorable with a wry commentary.
    forget

....

6   I'm going to use a real knife.
    imitation

....

7   Why knuckle under to male violence when you can tear off his ear?
    reason

....

8   It takes only the same strength as folding the Guardian in half.
    more

....

9   You don't need bulk if you can use your limbs as levers.
    unnecessary

....

10   Some ideas seem so obvious that it is surprising most women are unaware of
    them.
    such

....

Oral and written practice

Picture discussion
Look at the three pictures below, and then answer the questions which follow.

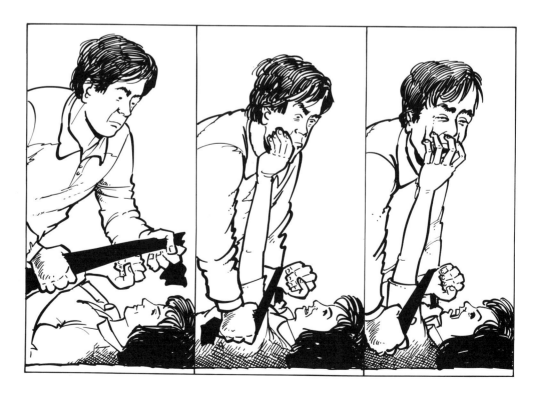

126

1 Describe what is happening in each of these pictures.
2 Do you think the man is winning? Why/why not?
3 How is the woman resisting, and what is she trying to do with her left hand?
4 Would you be able to defend yourself adequately in this sort of attack?
5 Do you think that it is possible for most women to fight on equal physical terms with men? Give reasons.

Communication activity

Look at one of the communication activities (4 or 14) at the back of the book. Read the news report and then tell your partner about it in your own words. Tell him/her what your opinion is and ask for his/her comments.

Written work

1   WOMAN BEATS OFF MUGGERS

 Write the newspaper report to which this headline refers.
 (about 300 words)

2 'Instead of trying to emulate men physically, women should concentrate on the things they are naturally good at.' Discuss. (about 350 words)

Unit 20

A Female Reaction

Reading comprehension

You will find after the following passage a number of statements, each with four
suggested endings. Choose the answer which you think fits best.

'You think I gave myself that cut, don't you? Three stitches are in there. I'd like you
to see it.'

'But I don't, I don't think you gave yourself it.' I had no idea what I thought.

'I was watching you when Cliff told you Steve had said he didn't know anything
5 about it and you stood there weighing it up. Weighing it up.'

'I wasn't, there were just some things I couldn't help—'

'You believe what somebody says your deranged, deluded, bloody raving maniac
of a son said instead of what your wife tells you happened. You see what that makes
me, don't you?'

10 'I don't believe—'

'Or rather what it reveals about what you think of me. You think I'm so neurotic,
so self-centred, so . . . unprincipled that I'd expose that boy, that poor madman to
being locked up and Christ knows what and I'd put you through it and suffer all that
pain myself just to . . . just for what? Attention? Is that what I was after?' She spoke in
15 the same level tone.

At least I had the sense to see that this was a question with no good answers.

'And you think I'd do that. As well as tell a lie on that scale. That seems to me about
the worst insult one person can give another. And I'm not having it.' She stood up.
'I'm off. And I'm not waiting till the morning as your friend suggests, I'm leaving
20 straight away. Catch me hanging on here with someone who thinks I'm like that.'

I stood up too. 'You're not fit to travel, you need rest,' I said, and got out of her way
as she moved towards the door.

'I'll risk it.' At the door she stopped and turned round. 'If anybody wants me they
can get me at my mother's. Though you'll be wasting your time if you try me there
25 yourself. I suppose you think that's funny. Yer, ass right, the wife's gorn orf to er
muvver's,' she said in a very poor imitation of perhaps a Hackney or Bow accent as
much as anything. 'Just up your street, you lower-class creep. I don't know how I've
put up with you for so long, with your gross table-manners and your boozing and
your bloody little car and your frightful mates and your whole ghastly south-of-the-
30 river man's world. You've no breeding and so you've no respect for women. They're

there to cook your breakfast and have sex with and that's it. So of course nothing they say's worth taking seriously, and when one of them says something quite important and serious and a man says something different then you believe him even though he's out of his mind. Oh, I wish to Christ I'd found out about you sooner.'

1 The passage seems to be from
   A   a women's liberation pamphlet.
   B   a work of fiction.
   C   a marriage guidance brochure.
   D   a radio documentary.

2 The woman seems to be most upset about
   A   the fact that her word is doubted.
   B   the fact that she has cut herself.
   C   the man's opinion of her.
   D   being neurotic.

3 The woman imitates another accent
   A   because she despises people from Hackney and Bow.
   B   to make the man respect her.
   C   to show her contempt for the man's social origins.
   D   because she is upset.

4 'You'll be wasting your time if you try me there yourself' (lines 24–25) means
   A   I won't speak to you if you call my mother's.
   B   I won't speak to you if you call at my mother's.
   C   Nobody will open the door if you call at my mother's.
   D   Nobody will answer the phone at my mother's house if you call.

5 According to the passage, which of the following is true?
   A   Someone has wounded the woman with a knife.
   B   She wants a divorce.
   C   The man regards women as slaves.
   D   The man isn't sure how the woman was injured.

Vocabulary
Explain the meaning of the following words and phrases as used in the passage.

   1   stitches (l 1)
   2   weighing it up (l 5)
   3   deranged (l 7)
   4   deluded (l 7)
   5   raving maniac (l 7)
   6   You see what that makes me (l 8–9)
   7   self-centred (l 12)
   8   locked up (l 13)
   9   I'd put you through it (l 13)
   10 Is that what I was after? (l 14)
   11 a lie on that scale (l 17)
   12 I'm not having it (l 18)
   13 I'm off (l 19)
   14 Catch me hanging on here (l 20)

15 not fit to travel (l 21)
16 they can get me at my mother's (ll 23–24)
17 Just up your street (l 27)
18 creep (l 27)
19 gross table-manners (l 28)
20 boozing (l 28)
21 frightful mates (l 29)
22 ghastly (l 29)
23 You've no breeding (l 30)
24 and that's it (l 31)
25 out of his mind (l 34)

Use of English

A Fill each of the blanks in the following passages with a suitable phrase.

> EXAMPLE: ....tennis in that heat, you would have been exhausted.
> ANSWER: *If you had played . . .*

1 'Not enough of a motive?' His voice had gone high. Messing up a man? Not enough of a motive? What are you talking about? Good God, ... (1) wives, haven't you? And not impossibly had some acquaintance with other women as well? You can't be new to feeling the edge of the most powerful weapon in their armoury. You .... (2) suffered before from the effect of their having noticed, at least the brighter ones among them having noticed, that men are different, men quite often wonder .... (3) doing the right thing and worry about it, men have been known to blame themselves for behaving badly, men .... (4) they've made mis- takes but on occasion will actually admit having done so, and say they're sorry, and ask to be forgiven, and promise .... (5) again, and mean it. Think of that! Mean it. All beyond female comprehension.'

2 Cliff was looking thoughtful. '.. .... (6) bloke on the telly the other night,' he said, 'twenty-five per cent of violent crime in England and Wales is husbands assaulting wives. Amazing figure that, don't you think? You'd expect it .... (7) like eighty per cent. Just goes to show what an easy-going lot English husbands are, only one in four of them .... (8) wife. No, it doesn't mean that, does it? But it's funny about wife-battering. Nobody ever even asks what the wife .... (9) or saying. She's never anything but an ordinary God-fearing woman who .... (10) have a battering husband.'

B For each of the sentences below, write a new sentence as similar as possible in meaning to the original sentence, but using the word given in **bold** letters. This word **must not be altered** in any way.

EXAMPLE: It wasn't my intention to frighten you.
mean
ANSWER: *I didn't mean to frighten you.*

1   You think I gave myself that cut.
    inflicted
    ....

2   I had no idea what I thought.
    think
    ....

3   You believe what someone else says rather than what your wife tells you.
    word
    ....

4   I had the sense to see that this was a question without an answer.
    realised
    ....

5   You're not fit to travel, you need rest.
    state
    ....

6   You'll be wasting your time if you try me there yourself.
    bother
    ....

7   You've no breeding and so you've no respect for women.
    due
    ....

8   Nothing they say is worth taking seriously.
    point
    ....

9   You believe him even though he's out of his mind.
    in spite
    ....

10 I wish I'd found out about you sooner.
    only
    ....

Oral and written practice

Written work
1   'The high divorce rate in some countries is due to most marriages being based on mutual misunderstanding.' Discuss. (about 350 words)
2   Write a description of the most interesting person of the opposite sex you have ever met. (about 350 words)

Picture discussion
Look at the cartoon below and answer these questions.

1 What is the situation depicted in the cartoon?
2 How would you describe the moods of the two people in the cartoon?
3 Do you find the cartoon humorous?
4 Do you think this cartoon suggests anything contained in the text at the beginning of this unit?
5 Do you think this is an accurate reflection of marriage? Why/why not?

"I'll meet you from work, then. How will I recognise you?"

Discussion topic
The following statements have all been made about women by men. What do you think each statement implies?

It is because of men that women dislike each other.

Ask a man for his opinion of women in general. His answer will tell you a lot about his wife.

Most women are not so young as they are painted.

Wild horses couldn't drag a secret out of most women. Unfortunately, women seldom have lunch with wild horses.

Women's intuition is the result of millions of years of not thinking.

Test 4   Units 16–20   (30 minutes)

Choose the word or phrase which best completes each sentence. Indicate your answer by putting the letter A, B, C or D in the space in each sentence.

1   The management has been promising a(n) .... in salary for ages, but nothing has happened.
    A   raising   B   rise   C   augmentation   D   growth
2   He arrived late at work and gave his boss a lame ....
    A   apology   B   reason   C   excuse   D   argument
3   In some countries, people who are dissatisfied with the political system are too frightened to .... out.
    A   speak   B   tell   C   protest   D   shout
4   If you don't ask for more money than you think you'll get, you've no room to ....
    A   argue   B   discuss   C   negotiate   D   compromise
5   He felt .... to work for aristocracy.
    A   profited   B   privileged   C   benefited   D   advantaged
6   Because the majority of people are apathetic, it is difficult to bring .... a social revolution.
    A   round   B   up   C   forward   D   about
7   Whose side are you .... ? Ours or theirs?
    A   with   B   for   C   in   D   on
8   If the workers want to improve their working conditions and terms of service, they will have to show ....
    A   solidarity   B   solidity   C   union   D   togetherness
9   The .... of a general strike would be impossible to calculate exactly.
    A   repercussions   B   rebounds   C   issues   D   outcomes
10 Considering that her son-in-law was not good enough for her daughter, the snobbish woman displayed a frigid .... towards him.
    A   enmity   B   bitterness   C   hostility   D   opposition
11 It is rather naive to accept everything at face ....
    A   surface   B   appearance   C   value   D   worth
12 The advice I gave him was .... ; he took no notice.
    A   indistinct   B   inefficient   C   ineffective   D   indiscernible
13 Most people are .... to flattery.
    A   sensible   B   susceptible   C   affected   D   impressionable
14 If only he weren't so self- .... ; he never considers anyone else.
    A   centred   B   sufficient   C   conscious   D   effacing
15 He's really clumsy; he can't .... bumping into things.
    A   help   B   prevent   C   refrain   D   resist
16 'You're overweight. Go .... a diet,' said the doctor.
    A   to   B   on   C   through   D   for
17 There has been no .... improvement in his behaviour since he got an official warning.
    A   persisting   B   durable   C   enduring   D   lasting
18 When she fell ill, she preferred not to see a doctor; she had lost .... in them.
    A   loyalty   B   devotion   C   faith   D   reliance
19 We should try to .... his attention from his problems.
    A   deviate   B   divert   C   diverge   D   divide
20 Success or failure in gambling all boils .... luck in the end.
    A   away from   B   over to   C   down to   D   down on

21 Members of a network are there to .... their own careers by helping each other.
A farther   B further   C feather   D follow

22 If you want to learn English, you must .... in mind that it would be better to go to an English-speaking country.
A bear   B take   C have   D carry

23 She's all .... her husband helping her with the housework.
A about   B for   C towards   D after

24 .... the boys are allowed to do engineering, the girls are forced to do domestic science.
A Yet   B However   C Despite   D While

25 He left his car on a hill without putting the brake on, and it ran over him! Can you .... that for stupidity?
A exceed   B improve   C better   D beat

26 Most women are .... to male dominance.
A contented   B conciliated   C settled   D reconciled

27 Many English words are .... from Latin and Greek.
A based   B derived   C founded   D originated

28 He works as an accountant, and says he has few .... to meet interesting people.
A occasions   B opportunities   C openings   D outlets

29 He .... himself in the exam: he got a grade 'A'.
A exceeded   B passed   C surpassed   D overtook

30 He has no .... to work so hard.
A necessity   B need   C obligation   D requirement

31 When the dentist told him he would have to have a tooth out, he .... himself to go through with it.
A steeled   B strengthened   C hardened   D ironed

32 After the fight, he was covered in ....
A blues   B bruises   C scars   D injuries

33 Everyone borrows money from him; he's an easy ....
A touch   B contact   C lender   D victim

34 Since the redundancies, the remaining staff just can't .... with the extra work-load.
A handle   B cope   C manage   D succeed

35 The workers want to know what they .... to gain if they accept the management's new proposals.
A suppose   B start   C stop   D stand

36 His teaching style is a .... between the autocratic and the permissive.
A mixture   B mix   C cross   D join

37 In the army, soldiers are expected to knuckle .... the strict discipline.
A down to   B down with   C under to   D under with

38 He has .... a new technique in self-defence.
A schemed   B managed   C contrived   D devised

39 When he was attacked in the dark street, he managed to fight off his ....
A assailants   B attacks   C assassins   D assaults

40 He had to have ten .... in the cut.
A stings   B sticks   C stickers   D stitches

41 Before you drink and drive, you should weigh .... the possible consequences.
A down   B in   C against   D up

42 'I'd prefer not to hurt you. It's your money I'm .... ,' said the mugger.
A into   B for   C after   D towards

43 'You're not .... to play – not with that injured leg', said the trainer.
   A fit   B good   C apt   D capable
44 He tried to do a(n) .... of an upper-class accent.
   A taking-off   B imitation   C copy   D likeness
45 He must be out of his .... if he thinks I'm going to work for nothing.
   A sense   B brain   C mind   D head
46 He's not really a friend; more of a(n) .... really.
   A intimate   B familiar   C acquaintance   D mate
47 He has been .... to make the right decision from time to time.
   A known   B considered   C believed   D thought
48 You must try to .... him for his rudeness.
   A forget   B forgive   C acquit   D overlook
49 Why they don't ban all cigarette advertising is .... my
   comprehension.
   A above   B beyond   C below   D over
50 He never loses his temper; he's very ....
   A easy-living   B easy-going   C easy-tempered   D easy-minded

Communication Activities

1   Read the story below and then tell your partners about it in your own words. Ask them for their comments.

> ONE THING the British upper class has always managed to do is to combine irresponsibility with a certain style.
>
> Take, for instance, the recent case of a young man from a well-off family in Berkshire who is quite incapable of keeping his bank balance anywhere near the black.
>
> Natural tact, apart from anything else, forbids me to name this chap, but suffice to say that his bank manager stoically endured his customer's profligacy for a long time. Finally he could stand it no longer, and summoned the young man to his office.
>
> The rake strolled in and eased himself into the chair opposite the bank manager's desk.
>
> "Do you realise," demanded the manager, "that your overdraft is currently running at twice my annual salary?"
>
> Truly shocked, the young man sat bolt upright in his chair.
>
> "Good God!" he exclaimed. "Have you ever thought of changing your job?"

2   The following passage is from a newspaper article. Your partners have other paragraphs from the same article. Read out your part of the article to the others and try to piece together the complete story.

> "I have been a very lucky and happy man, but it is only now that I have won all this money that I have realised it.
>
> "For all my life, I lived in the hope that something would happen to change my fortune, and that I would escape the poverty trap. That kept me going, or at least I thought it did. Now I realise I was very wrong."

3

> HEREFORD & WORCESTER
> PROBATION COMMITTEE
> Upper Norgrove Probation Hostel
>
> ## Housekeeper/Life Skills Teacher
>
> Upper Norgrove Hostel aims to help young adult delinquents to learn more successful ways of managing their lives. This post is one of six on the staff team and involves two main responsibilities – helping the residents to learn to look after themselves (cooking, budgeting, hygiene, etc) and taking responsibility for the smooth running of the domestic side of the hostel. The work is mainly done in normal office hours and does not entail living on the premises.
>
> The salary scale is £6,900–£7,713 per annum.
>
> If you are interested in this demanding but satisfying work, please write for further details to the Chief Probation Officer, Hereford & Worcester Probation Service, 3/4 Shaw Street, Worcester WR1 3QQ, enclosing a stamped addressed envelope. Completed application forms must be returned by July 14 (interviews: July 28).

4 Read the news report below and then tell your partner about it in your own words. Tell him/her what you think and ask for his/her comments.

If you study the current world ranking for chess players, you'll find that no woman is listed in the top 300 players. And one-time world champion Bobby Fischer used to boast that he could 'give any woman a knight's odds' (a bit like a 10 metre start in a 100 metre race) and still wipe her off the board. The British Women's Chess Federation was formed in 1982 with the aim of encouraging more women and girls to take up the game and to get national bodies like the British Chess Federation to take women's chess more seriously.

One of Britain's up-and-coming players is Mandy Hepworth from Fittleworth in Sussex. At 17 she is set to achieve the title of International Women's Master before long, and if her rapid rate of improvement continues she'll go much further than that.

'It's true,' says Mandy, 'that in adult chess women are nowhere near the level of the men at the moment, but that's because there are so many more of them playing. I don't think they're inherently better. Part of the problem is boys' and men's attitude as well. They try to put you down if you're a girl and a chess player. They don't take you seriously. You have to try very hard to prove yourself.'

Susan Walker is 20, and an International Women's Master who is probably one of Britain's overall top 30 chess players, as well as being the first British woman professional. She agrees with Mandy Hepworth that male resistance is one of the major obstacles to girls making headway in chess. 'A lot of boys and men are really over-confident about playing against girls. I've even known them laugh at the moves I make. So it's nice to beat them. On the other hand I don't know whether women can concentrate on chess as well as men can. Susan reckons that a woman world champion isn't a real possibility.

Michèle Carvalho and Lizette Pereira from Coloma Convent Girls' School in Croydon would probably disagree with her.

Michèle and Lizette play for Surrey Girls, and they have very definite ideas about why girls' chess has been such a slow starter.

Principally, they think the game has developed a bad image. 'Chess has got very low status among a lot of girls. They think it's really boring and square, and the sort of game that only spotty boys or 60-year-old men play. That image should be changed.'

5 The following passage is from a newspaper article. Your partners have other paragraphs from the same article. Read out your part of the article to the others and try to piece together the complete story.

His son Andreas, 34, who is married and has two children, was also upset. "We could have set up a family business and splurged, with plenty of money still left over for my father to give to charity," he said. "We could have been happy."

But for Eleftherio happiness is a matter of interpretation. "Now that I've got rid of all that money and am back where I started, I feel much better. In fact, I feel like a million dollars," he said.

6 You will be given 10–15 minutes to read the following stories. One of them is complete; the other has some information missing. By asking your partner questions, fill in the missing information in your incomplete story. Then answer your partner's questions about your other story.

October 9, 1983.

GEORGE BEST has had an amazing operation in a kill-or-cure bid to end his drinking.

It means that if he has just a few sips of alcohol the former soccer star would be violently ill for hours.

A few glasses could kill him.
The operation involved the implanting of twelve pellets of the drug Antabuse around the stomach. The drug reacts instantly to alcohol.

George declared at his bankruptcy hearing earlier this year: "I am an alcoholic."

Yesterday, as he cuddled his beautiful blonde lover former Miss World Mary Stavin, he spoke for the first time about the operation.

George, 37, said: "It has changed my life—for good.

"Without it there would always be the danger that I might slip back into my bad old ways."

He added: "Just how many drinks it would take to kill me nobody knows for sure. But my doctor told me a full drinking bout would be fatal.

"The operation has taken a terrible weight off my shoulders and I feel great.

"At the same time there is this deadly sword hanging over me . . . and I'm the one who has put it there."

George travelled alone to Norway eleven days ago for the operation, which is rarely performed in Britain.

The doctor at the clinic in Oslo tried to talk him out of having it—for there have been cases of drinkers dying while on Antabuse.

George said: "He asked me again and again if I realised what I was doing and what would happen to me afterwards if I drank.

"I said I did and told him to go ahead."

Ten minutes later it was all over and George, who had the operation under local anaesthetic, paid a £20 fee and went back to his hotel. The next day he returned to Britain a new man.

At the love nest flat in Chelsea which he shares with 25-year-old Mary, George told of two incidents since the operation that have given him great encouragement.

He was travelling back to London when his train came to a sudden halt and was held up for an hour.

"I was really upset and the old George Best would have got off and found the nearest bar. But this time I just sat there," he said.

The second incident came a few days ago when he answered a knock on the door and found two girls advertising a new wine and asking him to sample it.

George said: "I just had to laugh and told them, 'I'd better not, or you will have a very sick man lying at your feet'."

George has brighter hopes for the future.

He said: "I have a keep fit record coming out with Mary and we are planning to set up a health centre."

He revealed he is also planning to write a novel.

November 4, 1984.

FALLEN soccer idol George Best was yesterday wanted by police with a warrant for his arrest.

He failed to turn up in court on a .... charge after being stopped while driving near Buckingham Palace early yesterday.

He was taken to Cannon Row police station and bailed to appear at Bow Street court later in the morning. But he still had not arrived when the case was called at 11.45 a.m.

Magistrate Mr William Robins raised his eyebrows and said: "No answer. My goodness. You'd better try to bring him in."

Two policemen waited outside the court to ....

But there was no sign of the wayward night-clubber when the court rose in the afternoon.

Police also went to the home in Oakley Street, Chelsea, which he shares with ....

But Best had left the flat and hailed a cab.

Later Best's manager Mr Bill McMurdo said: "I'm amazed at this news.

"George telephoned me .... and didn't mention anything about it." Best failed to turn up for ....

More than 200 guests were left kicking their heels while Best was said to be .... times Best has had drug pellets implanted in his stomach in a bid to beat alcoholism.

But he is said to be back on .... in spite of a 14-month battle against his problem.

Later Best returned to his flat supported by ....

Asked if he knew there was a warrant out for his arrest, he mumbled: ....

7 Read the two stories below and then tell your partners about them in your own words. Ask them for their comments.

AN ARAB prince has paid £95,000 for an English wood —so he can use it once a year for a picnic.

The Saudi multi-millionaire has never seen historic 40-acre Bullock Wood, near Colchester, Essex.

But after seeing a photograph of it he immediately agreed to pay the asking price.

He plans to fly in with his family for an annual picnic under the trees.

MISS CANNON IS NO SNIP!

HEAVEN knows how lovely Hollywood star Dyan Cannon's hair will look when she gets married next weekend, but it's a cinch that the nuptial hair-do won't cost anything like what British TV bosses paid for a haircut Dyan never even had.

The staggering cost of flying in her personal hairdresser from America and then keeping him on hand throughout the 11 weeks of filming a four hour mini-series called Jennie's War was £76,000.

What amazed everyone was when Ms Cannon realised that her role in the wartime thriller called on her to have short-cropped hair.

"She refused to have her hair cut even by her own hairdresser," said Harlech TV producer Peter Graham Scott. "We had to have a series of expensive wigs made."

He added: "I don't know why she wanted her own hairdresser brought over anyway."

Ms Cannon's financial demands were hefty, too— more than enough to push the boat out when the former Mrs Cary Grant weds Stanley Fimberg aboard a yacht in Los Angeles.

The 46-year-old star picked up a £400,000 fee.

8 The following passage is from a newspaper article. Your partners have other paragraphs from the same article. Read out your part of the article to the others and try to piece together the complete story.

But his win has made him realise that money had never been his real object in life after all.

In fact he realised he preferred to be poor and live in hope.

So he has given all the money he won to charity.

"I just didn't enjoy being rich," he said. "For all the years I've been poor I haven't been unhappy. Perhaps this surprises some people. I've never had a serious quarrel with my wife Sofia. And I have always been honest.

"I brought my sons up to be honest and hard working, and now both have good jobs with shipping companies. I have wonderful friends who like me not because of my money or social status but simply because they enjoy my company.

9 You will be given 10–15 minutes to read the following stories. One of them is complete; the other has some information missing. By asking your partner questions, fill in the missing information in your incomplete story. Then answer your partner's questions about your other story.

October 9, 1983.

GEORGE BEST has had an amazing operation in a kill-or-cure bid to ....

It means that if he has just a few sips of alcohol the former soccer star would ....
....

A few glasses could kill him. The operation involved ....
....

The drug reacts instantly to
....
....

George declared at his bankruptcy hearing earlier this year: "I am an alcoholic."

Yesterday, as he cuddled
....
....,
he spoke for the first time about the operation.

George, 37, said: "It has changed my life—for good.

"Without it there would always be the danger that I might slip back into my bad old ways."

He added: "Just how many drinks it would take to kill me nobody knows for sure. But my doctor told me
....
....

"The operation has taken a terrible weight off my shoulders and I feel great.

"At the same time there is this deadly sword hanging over me . . . and I'm the one who has put it there."

George travelled alone to Norway eleven days ago for the operation, which is rarely performed in Britain.

The doctor at the clinic in Oslo tried to talk him out of having it—for ....
....

George said: "He asked me again and again if I realised what I was doing and what would happen to me afterwards if I drank.

"I said I did and told him to go ahead."

Ten minutes later it was all over and George, who had the operation under local anaesthetic, paid a £20 fee and went back to his hotel. The next day he returned to Britain a new man.

At the love nest flat in Chelsea which he shares with ....
.... ,
George told of two incidents since the operation that have given him great encouragement.

He was travelling back to London when his train came to a sudden halt and was held up for an hour.

"I was really upset and the old George Best would have ....
....
But this time I just sat there," he said.

The second incident came a few days ago when he answered a knock on the door and found two girls advertising a new wine and asking him to sample it.

George said: "I just had to laugh and told them, ...
....

George has brighter hopes for the future.

He said: "I have a keep fit record coming out with Mary and we are planning
....
....

He revealed he is also planning to write a novel.

November 4, 1984.

FALLEN soccer idol George Best was yesterday wanted by police with a warrant for his arrest.

He failed to turn up in court on a breath-test charge after being stopped while driving near Buckingham Palace early yesterday.

He was taken to Cannon Row police station and bailed to appear at Bow Street court later in the morning. But he still had not arrived when the case was called at 11.45 a.m.

Magistrate Mr William Robins raised his eyebrows and said: "No answer. My goodness. You'd better try to bring him in."

Two policemen waited outside the court to arrest the 38-year-old former Manchester United star.

But there was no sign of the wayward night-clubber when the court rose in the afternoon.

Police also went to the home in Oakley Street, Chelsea, which he shares with model girl Angie Lynn.

But Best had left the flat and hailed a cab.

Later Best's manager Mr Bill McMurdo said: "I'm amazed at this news.

"George telephoned me at 7 a.m. and didn't mention anything about it." Best failed to turn up for his benefit dinner in Manchester two weeks ago.

More than 200 guests were left kicking their heels while Best was said to be celebrating at Blondes, his new night-spot in London.

Three times Best has had drug pellets implanted in his stomach in a bid to beat alcoholism.

But he is said to be back on the booze in spite of a 14-month battle against his problem.

Later Best returned to his flat supported by a blonde and a brunette.

Asked if he knew there was a warrant out for his arrest, he mumbled: "Is there?"

10 The following passage is from a newspaper article. Your partners have other paragraphs from the same article. Read our your part of the article to the others and try to piece together the complete story.

> **ATHENS:** Eleftherio Veniamin had never had much money, but he had always worked hard and lived in the hope that one day fortune would smile on him.
>
> He and his wife had raised two sons in Piraeus where he worked on the ferries.
>
> But the boys never had new shoes or fashionable clothes and his wife had never bought a dress from a shop—she made all the dresses she ever wore.

11

> **NORTH WEST LONDON HOUSING ASSOCIATION in conjunction with MIDDLESEX AREA PROBATION SERVICE**
>
> # ALCOHOL PROJECT
>
> North West London Housing Association in partnership with Middlesex area Probation Service has set up a project in Haringey for problem drinkers.
> The project provides assessment, social work care, onward referral, as well as temporary accommodation for problem drinkers referred by the probation service and other agencies.
> N.W.L.H.A. requires a PROJECT WORKER to join a team of nine staff who provide the service to clients. Relevant work/life experience more important than qualifications.
> Salary scale 5 S.P. 23. £8,847 p.a. including London weighting (under review). In addition a sleep-in allowance of £10.59 per night is paid.
> For further information and application form please contact the Manager, Paddy Costall, N.W.L.H.A. Alcohol Project (Haringey), 530–532 West Green Road, London N15 3DX, Telephone 01-888 7737. Closing date 18th July. Interviews 5th August.
> *Applications are welcome irrespective of gender, race or religious beliefs.*

Leisure Department

ATHLETICS MOTIVATOR

Robin Park Athletics Stadium, Wigan

Grade NJC Scale 5 £7,920–£8,697

— Two-year fixed-term contract — (in the first instance)

For the promotion, organisation and development of athletics at this prestigious athletics stadium, which has been designated the Regional Athletics Resources Centre, and is the major competitive venue in the region. The Grade I outdoor facilities are augmented by superb training facilities within the 1,000 seats spectator stand, which also contains meeting rooms and the appropriate audio visual equipment.

You will be responsible to the Chief Leisure Officer and will be required to liaise with Education Authorities, Local and Regional Athletics bodies, Regional and National Coaches and Officers and other organisations intent in the pursuit of athletics excellence.

You will work 36¼ hours per week, some of which will apply to evenings and weekends.

For further information and an application form please write to: Chief Personnel Officer, Civic Centre, Millgate, Wigan, or ring our 24-hour answering service on Wigan 42472 and leave your name and address — please state which job you are interested in. Closing date: 18th July.

METROPOLITAN
WIGAN

THE LONDON DOLPHINARIUM
urgently needs an

ACQUA MAID

Must be – an excellent swimmer
– attractive
– fond of animals

This is a full-time appointment.
For further information contact
M. Trainer on 01-541 6666

GACARA

GREENWICH ACTION COMMITTEE
AGAINST RACIST ATTACKS

TWO RACIAL HARASSMENT WORKERS
(FULL-TIME)
SALARY SCALE 6 + OLW + 10% UNSOCIAL HOURS

We are a racist attack and police monitoring group based in Woolwich. We are looking for two workers to join our existing team. Both workers will be expected to do casework and to continue existing projects around estates policing and youth. One of the workers will require at least one Asian language and knowledge of working within the black community are both essential requirements for all applicants.

FOR FURTHER DETAILS PLEASE RING
01-854 4587 and ask for MR. UPPAL

CLOSING DATE FOR APPLICATIONS:
1st NOVEMBER

12 The following passage is from a newspaper article. Your partners have other paragraphs from the same article. Read out your part of the article to the others and try to piece together the complete story.

> "I never knew what it was like to splash out on the luxuries of life," said Eleftherio, now 70 and retired. "I never had enough money left over from my wages to spend on any extras. Just the food, electricity and basics used up all the money I took home."
>
> But he did allow himself one extravagance. For more than 50 years he regularly bought tickets for the Greek national lottery.
>
> Now one £1.50 ticket has won him almost £1 million.

13 Read the story below and then tell your partners about it in your own words. Ask them for their comments.

> He was a coward and knew it. He hadn't been able to say no to his father's millions, or to his factory, his shops and his hundreds of employees. He was the heir; his life was already mapped out.
>
> One day, he succeeded to this business empire specialising in garden furniture, parasols, imitation stone statues and garden gnomes. The gnomes had become the emblem of the company, and just thinking of them made him quiver with hatred.
>
> He really wanted to be an artist and hadn't put much effort into his studies. However, a succession of private teachers, expensive schools and periods spent abroad had pushed and dragged him up to the minimum acceptable level.
>
> Once, he had tried to rebel. For six months he had wandered around the world, living from day to day. His father had cut off his allowance, knowing who would submit first.
>
> Sure enough, the son submitted. He couldn't do without his luxury car, his flat crammed with gadgets or the mountains of money which made his existence so cosy.
>
> His father made him head of a department and gave him a vast office, where he was bored from the first day, he had nothing to do, and his subordinates despised him. Inside, he seethed with rage but he kept it bottled up: he was a coward and accepted the situation.
>
> However, he had a secret which kept him going. Each morning, before leaving his luxury house in his big car, he went down to the cellar. There, with an almost unbelievable violence, he smashed a dozen or so of his factory's garden gnomes against a wall.

14 Read the news report below and then tell your partner about it in your own words. Tell him/her what you think about it and ask for his/her comments.

SALLY CLINE and Dale Spender were sitting in a London restaurant when they started to take note of the way women treated men.

To begin with, they realised women smiled at men far more than men smiled at women.

They smiled at the men they were with, they smiled at the waiters, one woman even smiled at a man who blundered into her path—and she was the one who apologised to him.

Two women eating together were interrupted by a man who asked them to join him and his friend since they were dining "alone".

Even as they turned him down, they smiled because "we didn't want him to feel badly about it."

The discovery set Cline and Spender thinking, researching and then writing a book. In it they examine the way women the world over work hard to make men feel good.

Of course, there are all kinds of reasons why women go on massaging men's egos. To keep the peace, to keep a job, to keep a husband. And there is no doubt that when women stop playing the game the result can be alarming.

In 1970 New York receptionists operated a smile boycott. For one week they simply refused to smile.

Dale says: "There was one disaster after another. It was not just the immediate and interminable queries of 'what's wrong with you?', although these responses were significant enough and difficult to handle.

"Some men got abusive—wildly so. Receptionists were accused of ruining the day of many a man, of deliberate sabotage, and cases of physical threats were not uncommon."

15 The following passage is from a newspaper article. Your partners have other paragraphs from the same article. Read out your part of the article to the others and try to piece together the complete story.

But Mr Veniamin's family do not share his point of view, and he may be facing the first quarrel with his wife in 40 years of marriage.

"I think he's gone a bit potty," said 64-year-old Sofia. "We've always been happy, but we always looked forward to a time when we could go on a spree. This was our last chance. Now that my husband has given all the money away, I can't even buy myself a dress from a shop."

Answer Key

Reading comprehension (p. 7)

First passage
1B   2A   3C   4C   5C   6B

Second passage
7D   8C   9A   10B

Use of English (p. 9)

A

1 to	11 very/also
2 phenomenon/thing/fact	12 Thirdly/Lastly/Moreover
3 century	13 not
4 real/understandable/	14 president
genuine/so	15 but/he
5 goes/runs/went/ran	16 costs
6 else	17 money/cash
7 over/around	18 something/whatever
8 real	19 in
9 than	20 come
10 man/person/chap	

B

1   It was the first time (that) a monarch had (ever) walked about among the crowds.
2   It is thirty-four years since she began to rule/her rule.
    It is thirty-four years since she came to the throne.
3   As far as the Queen was concerned, her coronation was a deeply religious experience.
4   The Duchess of Norfolk was asked/requested/persuaded/made/obliged   to do her rehearsing for her.
5   Hate letters are sent to/received by   anyone who says anything disparaging about royals.
6   Indoctrination is a process which/that   starts early.
7   Old-age pensioners lead worse lives than the royal horses.
8   Before (the start of) big rugby and football matches, brass-bands play the National Anthem.
9   No sooner had the film ended than everyone rushed to the exit.
    No sooner did the film end than everyone rushed to the exit.
10   The number of MPs who attend is fewer/less   than a dozen.

Reading comprehension (p. 12)

Suggested answers.
1   An authoritarian attitude.
2   Because such differences might seem to contradict the democratic ideal, one of the basic ideas of which is equality.

3 Inheritance.
4 He is happy to consider his personal situation as pre-destined/determined by an unchallengeable power.
5 The lowliest peasant.
6 Modern democracies.
7 A problem in the disposal of aggression.
8 Modern democracies moving away from the more primitive authoritarian/aristocratic pattern.
9 Be neglected/forgotten.
10 to emphasise the apparent contradiction that democracies (based on equality) support armies, whose structure is rigidly hierarchical and undemocratic.
11 'Uniform' means 'equal' or 'the same', and an officer's uniform is decorated with tabs or badges which indicate his superior status.
12 A violent attack in words by a sergeant-major on a soldier of inferior rank.
13 To make sure that he dare not question orders/has no alternative but to fight the enemy.
14 There would be no stability or unity, and therefore no uniform philosophy or concerted action.
15 There should be some kind of definition of the structure of democracy, based on **some** of the following ideas:
– government by majority (one man, one vote, etc.)
– equality of rights and respect for the rights of minorities
– freedom of speech and opinion; opposition between rival groups allowed
– division between those who govern and those who are governed is lessened.

The following points should also be mentioned:
– military structure demands strict hierarchy and total obedience to one's superiors, a system which allows a soldier to take it out on his inferiors
– unlike civilian clothing, military clothing has decorations distinguishing officers from ordinary soldiers
– military training indoctrinates soldiers with the idea that men are unequal; everyone knows his place
– in an army, it is essential for everyone to act together against a common enemy, whereas internal opposition is allowed in a democracy.

Use of English (p. 13)

A

1	become	11	Close/Thorough
2	our/all	12	out
3	arguments/ideas/justifications	13	equal
4	forward	14	same
5	as	15	with
6	completely/totally/largely/widely/etc.	16	system/structure
7	all/their/any/real	17	on
8	by	18	in
9	in	19	remains/stays/is
10	disappear/vanish/go	20	maintained/upheld/preserved

B

1 Despite every society recognising the need for leadership, democracy tries to have unauthoritarian leaders.
2 Inheritance later took the place of dominance.

3   The trend can be determined easily/without difficulty.
    The trend can easily be determined.
4   'Uniform' is an inappropriate name/word   for the dress of soldiers/soldiers' dress.
5   It is said that Frederick II insisted that a soldier must fear his officer more than the enemy.
6   This hierarchical structure makes for a stable society.
    This hierarchical structure makes things/society   more stable.
7   All political power has been taken (away) from the monarchies that survive.
8   The great millenium has turned into a political reality.
9   The supposition that all men are equal is a fallacy.
10 The spread of education has replaced the old class system with a new one.

Unit 3

Reading comprehension (p. 16)

Correct sequence: **b   d   a   e   c**

Vocabulary
*Teachers might like to indicate in this and later units the vocabulary that would generally be regarded as more colloquial.

a
1   down-to-earth
2   ultra-glam* (glam = glamorous)
3   tottering
4   low-key
5   flaunt
6   thrifty
7   a taboo subject
8   dig into
9   skinny-dipping*
10 moping

b
1   lurking
2   with silver spoons in their mouths
3   within a stone's throw of
4   flock
5   rubbing shoulders with
6   lesser species
7   trilled
8   pressed up against
9   Hooray Henry*
10 jeopardise

c
1   hangover
2   revels
3   staggers
4   gossip
5   fortifies
6   giggle
7   buzzing through
8   booze*
9   stodge
10 fighting fit

d
1   disintegrate
2   capital
3   catch (on the hook)
4   handing down
5   darn
6   menial chores
7   brill* (brill = brilliant)
8   hunk*
9   carry . . . off
10 jazzed up*

e
1   running riot
2   scoffed
3   string . . . together
4   come out with
5   stunning
6   epitome
7   put up with
8   oblivious to
9   sneers
10 bearing

148

Use of English (p. 21)

A
1 They normally live in/inhabit   London's elegant Knightsbridge.
2 Were I (to be) pressed up against a Hooray Henry, it would be quite superb.
3 Because of her background and breeding, Katie has an impeccable Sloane pedigree.
4 At no time would she jeopardise her future comfort by falling in love with a working-class man.
5 Women have fallen at his feet throughout his life.
   Women have been falling at his feet throughout his life.
6 A wonderful aura and magnetism surround her.
7 A Sloane's life is so busy that it cannot/can't   be glamorous.
8 An ordinary man is much/far   less likely than a Sloane man to turn around.
9 Watered-down scrambled eggs and baked beans will be sufficient/enough (for us).
   Watered-down scrambled eggs and baked beans will do/suffice.
10 Ultimate fun to/for   a Sloane is spraying champagne at people.

B

1 who gave	6 when he met/came across
2 It wasn't the	7 I'll fight (you)
3 shouldn't have been	8 he did/tried his
4 did they get their/the	9 didn't (use to) go to/wouldn't go to
5 where they got	10 they're (all) in the

Unit 4

Reading comprehension (p. 24)

T = True, F = False, ? = Don't know.
1 F   2 T   3 ?   4 F   5 T
6 F   7 F   8 F   9 ?   10 ?
11 T   12 ?   13 T   14 T   15 ?

Vocabulary

A
1 do away with
2 highly-acclaimed
3 prospects
4 over-indulgence
5 mansion
6 income
7 currently
8 have a sense of isolation
9 deal with
10 elaborate

B
1 being born with wealth and privileges can bring problems/have negative effects (from the expression 'born with a silver spoon in your mouth')
2 inability to settle/stay in one place
3 all the possessions previously mentioned (royal estates, picture collections, etc.)

4 inherit the position/rank etc (of his father)
5 legal rights to extract minerals from a piece of land (in this case tin from the lands of the Duchy of Cornwall)
6 place where oysters are found at the bottom of the sea
7 unreal, extravagant environment
8 the chance of being born into a particular family
9 more of a problem /disadvantage   than a blessing
10 first/most important   consideration

Use of English (p. 26)

A

1	earns/makes	11	grew
2	more	12	off
3	Yet/But	13	up
4	such/this/his	14	to
5	Together/Along	15	do/admittedly
6	still	16	life
7	used	17	afford/have
8	other	18	do
9	with	19	running
10	time	20	so

B

1 It is the wealthy who most often commit suicide.
2 Dr Robert Coles knows more about this subject than anyone else in the world.
  Dr Robert Coles has more expertise in this subject than anyone else in the world.
3 The title of the/a   book he has written is 'The Privileged Ones'.
  'The Privileged Ones' is the title of the/a   book he has written.
  He has written a book with the title 'The Privileged Ones'.
4 Having so much to choose from is the cause of their confusion.
  The cause of their confusion is having so much to choose from.
5 Travelling around makes them/you/one/a person   feel restless.
6 I find it difficult/impossible   to imagine that Prince William will not be self-assured.
7 William will be the next Prince of Wales.
8 The Duchy is composed of 26,000 acres of Cornwall.
9 He will feel isolated.
10 They cannot feel inwardly satisfied about that.

Unit 5

Reading comprehension (p. 29)

Passage **a**
1C   2A

Passage **b**
3A   4B

Passage **c**
5B

Vocabulary

A

Passage **a**
1 well-heeled
2 fork out
3 infuriated
4 ritzy
5 boycotting
6 cocktail circuit
7 eyebrows are being raised
8 slammed

Passage **b**
9 reaped
10 staggering

11 newlywed
12 thumping*
13 superbitch*
14 furrier
15 lottery

Passage **c**
16 erupted
17 in the light of
18 have the neck to*
19 handout
20 prima donnas

B

Passage **a**
1 place frequently visited for holidays
2 an organised dance or entertainment whose profits are given to people in need
3 used selfishly, for one's own profit
4 photograph
5 permission
6 having high status
7 to support
8 money awarded to students

Passage **b**
1 a very brief visit
2 prize which increases in value until it is won
3 which can be calculated as
4 a television/radio show   on which a host/hostess   talks informally to guests (usually well-known)
5 payment
6 place where products for sale (in this case cars) are put on display.

Passage **c**
1 quarrel; argument; controversy
2 tried to persuade; strongly recommended
3 ridiculous; stupid
4 underprivileged; lacking basic necessities
5 surrenders; submits
6 pays too much

Use of English (p. 32)

A
1 A double ticket will cost other guests £7,000.
2 A family snapshot with the Prince and Princess is included in the meal ticket.
3 They can't possibly know/have any idea   this kind of thing is going on.
4 It is expected that film stars will attend.
5 £1,400,000 is what/how much/the sum/the amount   the organisers hope to raise.

£1,400,000 is the organisers' target.
6 5 hours is all/the time   it took Joan Collins to earn £85,930.
7 £20,000 is what Joan earned/collected   for presenting a cheque to a pools winner.
£20,000 was Joan's fee/payment   for presenting a cheque to a pools winner.
8 The first thing she did was (to) make a ten-minute appearance on a chat show.
9 Should the government give in, they'll be forced to pay £65 a year.
10 Shock is what millions of people will feel at this handout.
Shock will be the reaction of millions of people to this handout.

B
1 The rent-a-royal plan has made locals furious.
2 They are of the opinion that Charles and Diana are being exploited.
In their opinion, Charles and Diana are being exploited.
3 It is expected that stars such as Bob Hope will attend.
4 People/They   were anxious about/at   the amount of money raised.
5 She slammed the 'hard-sell' (of Charles and Diana) on the grounds of 'not being appropriate or polite'.
6 She earns £1,000 a minute for playing superbitch Alexis.
7 Her appearance on a chat show lasted ten minutes.
8 The last thing she did was (to) call at the Hilton Hotel to draw a winning lottery ticket.
9 Selina Scott's new contract has caused a row to erupt.
10 The BBC pays its prima donnas more than they are worth.

Oral and written practice

Communication activity
Correct sequence: 10, 12, 8, 2, 15, 5.

Unit 6

Reading comprehension (p. 38)

Suggested answers.
1 Perfected the gift/ability.
2 The influence on young tennis players of the bad sportsmanship and lack of self-control of established tennis stars like Becker and Nastase.
3 When the girl says, 'I don't care what the umpire says' (lines 18–19). When the Hungarian girl burst into tears after losing, and only after some time, and very reluctantly, congratulated her opponent.
4 Parents with exaggerated dreams for their children's success/who see their children as potential stars.
5 A situation where Mr Foldenyi has not just witnessed the tragic drama of his daughter losing a tennis match.
6 Yesterday/yesterday's tennis match.
7 A step up the ladder of success/a step on the way to becoming a champion.
8 To encourage love of tennis as a sport rather than love of fame and the business aspects.
9 To hit a tennis ball.
10 The International Tennis Federation.

11 The protective bandages/strapping around their knees make(s) many youngsters look like wounded soldiers from a battlefield.
12 Because the ETA are bound by an existing contract with the Walt Disney Organisation promoting junior tennis.
13 To persuade them to respect the limits, both physical and psychological, of young players, and not push them too hard.
14 The following points should be included:
  – young players imitate the bad-tempered behaviour of older players
  – nowadays, such behaviour is widely regarded as an inherent feature of being successful
  – over-ambitious coaches and parents putting excessive pressure on the youngsters
  – tennis is more of a business than a sport; the desire to win (and make money) overrides the pleasure of taking part
  – some youngsters suffer serious injury by playing too often
  – not enough is known about the pressures on young players; there is a need for more research.

Use of English (p. 40)

A

1	from	11	last
2	getting/becoming	12	with/to
3	poor	13	discover/learn/note
4	it	14	those
5	for	15	concerned
6	only/around/almost/over	16	than
7	expenses	17	up
8	off	18	it/them
9	to	19	therefore/consequently
10	hardly/not	20	Despite

B

1 I have watched as Ilie Nastase (completely) lost his temper.
2 I was horror-struck at what we have inherited from them.
3 I couldn't care less/give a damn (about) what the umpire says.
4 You/One didn't need to look/search too hard here to see the pressures of competition.
5 She burst into tears.
6 Only when she had wept for several minutes did she shake her opponent's hand.
7 Tennis is more (of) a business than a sport now.
8 They recently voted to make/declare it illegal for under-fourteens to play/compete on the professional circuit.
9 There is a plan to do away with international competition at under-twelve level.
10 The (big/great) danger comes from parents and coaches.

Unit 7

Reading comprehension (p. 43)

Correct sequence: **b c e d a**

Vocabulary

A

a
1 prevent
2 about to
3 take part
4 upset
5 torn apart

b
1 barbaric
2 controversial
3 elite
4 crawling
5 run

c
1 contribute
2 underprivileged
3 backed
4 outlaw
5 abandoned

d
1 inflict pain
2 mature
3 fans
4 pundit
5 act

e
1 petition
2 so-called
3 chased
4 slit
5 villains

B

a
1 too ridiculous for words
2 would not take a decision/commit themselves
3 he couldn't justify/give reasons in support of his opinions
4 should have learned from experience not to repeat the same mistakes
5 a group of people with a particular interest, who try to influence those in power

b
1 forbidden
2 firm; powerful; uncompromising
3 well-known, popular people who are also involved in football
4 controversial subject
5 the group of people who support/go hunting

c
1 or someone like that; a similar group
2 firm position/opinion
3 idiots; stupid people
4 stop it; give up doing it
5 the others would do the same soon afterwards

d
1 There is something (seriously) wrong with
2 fellow; man*
3 for any reason
4 strong; ruthless
5 take a decision; commit oneself

e
1 organise
2 is beginning to think/behave   sensibly
3 a slight feeling of regret/compassion/remorse
4 incomprehensible (to me)
5 let it go; release it

Use of English (p. 46)

A
1 Were we all to behave like that, there wouldn't be anything living on this island.
2 It is possible to stop the hunters.
3 'Off' was the second of the two words I said to them.
4 Providing Neil Kinnock gets to Downing Street, the Labour Party will outlaw foxhunting.
5 Unless the Royals stop soon, I'm going to get up a petition to shoot corgis.
6 I don't understand the mentality of the people who do it.
7 The last thing I could do is (to) shoot a pheasant.
   The last thing I could do would be (to) shoot a pheasant.
8 If only every fox in the country could run as fast as he did.
9 I find it unbelievable/incredible   that there is a Royal society to prevent cruelty to animals when the Royal Family go hunting and shooting.
   I find it unbelievable/incredible   that a Royal society exists to prevent cruelty to animals when the Royal Family go hunting and shooting.
10 The number of people who take part in hunting , shooting and fishing is five and a half million.

B
1 cannot/can't   understand/imagine
2 be described
3 of fear of/they fear/they are afraid of/they are frightened of
4 though/if   you are
5 place in the
6 see/regard/consider   hunting/it
7 habit of; reputation of
8 is keeping/to keep   the
9 were (to be) banned
10 (straight) for the (fox's)

Oral and written practice (p. 47)

Discussion topic
a Someone who goes hunting – possibly being interviewed for radio/newspaper, etc.
b Someone involved in anti-hunting activities or in a related organisation – possibly being interviewed for radio/newspaper, etc.
c Written narrative, taken from a novel.
d Description (written) of an aristocrat's hunting/shooting activities – possibly the writer disapproves, as there is a slightly ironic element throughout the paragraph.

Unit 8

Reading comprehension (p. 50)

T = True, F = False, ? = Don't know.
 1 F 2 F 3 T 4 F 5 ?
 6 T 7 T 8 F 9 T 10 F
11 ? 12 T 13 ? 14 T 15 F

Vocabulary

A

1	broken down	6	pick up
2	carry on	7	things are too soft
3	witnessed	8	takes effect
4	confiscated	9	resigning
5	broken in	10	witty

B
 1 resigned; given up; left
 2 to explain why (he is leaving)
 3 drew quickly and roughly
 4 tolerate; bear; put up with
 5 cut (deeply and violently)
 6 knife with a hidden blade which jumps out when a button on the handle is pressed
 7 older pupils in a school with authority over other children
 8 support; co-operation
 9 physical punishment (e.g. caning, beating)
10 a person authorised to express the opinions of a group/organisation

Use of English (p. 51)

A
 1 His sketch showed/depicted   children fighting, drinking and smoking.
 2 There has been a complete breakdown of discipline.
 3 McIntyre has witnessed an increase in violence among the pupils.
 4 My car tyres have been slashed.
 5 The teachers are sworn at by kids.
 6 I feel it would be a good idea/desirable   to bring the cane back.
   I feel it is time to bring the cane back.
 7 It is a year since the present headmaster joined the school.
 8 I have no wish to comment further.
   I have nothing more to say.
   I have no further comment (to make).
 9 In spite of McIntyre's cartoon being witty, it is totally unrealistic.
   In spite of the fact that McIntyre's cartoon is witty, it is totally unrealistic.
10 We do not regard discipline at Amery Hill as a problem

B

1	deal of	6	had kicked/punched/hit
2	(as) a teacher	7	should/can I (possibly) do
3	it is at	8	time/day I took it to
4	do they regard/view/treat	9	away with
5	up a fight	10	against those/pupils/students who

Unit 9

Reading comprehension (p. 56)

First passage
1C 2C 3B 4D 5C

Second passage
6B 7C 8A 9D 10A

Use of English (p. 59)

A

1 how
2 on/upon/over
3 place
4 as
5 with
6 make/have
7 adopt/follow/use
8 our
9 what
10 students/pupils

11 to
12 consistent
13 fulfil
14 treated/regarded/seen/viewed
15 failures
16 works/functions
17 Students/Pupils/Those
18 way/manner
19 It
20 very/selfsame/whole

B

1 The principal need/desire   of the average human being is security.
2 If man is committed to (certain) objectives, he will exercise self-control in their service.
3 Not only does the average human being learn to accept responsibility, but he also learns to seek it.
   Not only does the average human being learn to accept responsibility, but also to seek it.
4 These strategies will make him able to exercise constant surveillance over their work.
   These strategies will make it possible for him to exercise constant surveillance over their work.
5 Resistance, apathy and minimum effort will be the result(s)/effect(s)/consequence(s)   of coercing a student to learn.
   Resistance, apathy and minimum effort will result from/be caused by   coercing a student to learn.
6 This is both naive and untrue.
7 If the conditions are right, many people will find sufficient satisfaction in their work.
   If people are given the right conditions, they will find satisfaction in their work.
8 It is up to (the) teachers to set up the right conditions for this to happen.
9 The way to harness student motivation is by enriching the learning experience.
10 It appears/seems (that) less successful teachers are restricted to a limited number of roles.

Unit 10

Reading comprehension (p. 62)
Suggested answers.
 1 Someone who has a passionate belief which he feels he must communicate to as many people as possible.
 2 Not easy to understand the significance of.
    A wide variety of subjects.
 3 The fact that she studied a broad range of subjects.
 4 Her enormous interest in her subject.
 5 Because they thought she was too advanced for a normal school curriculum.
 6 Encouraging her to find things out for herself by using a series of questions and answers.
 7 He has never preached his own ideas dogmatically.
 8 He was never pushed intellectually; the pace of learning was too slow.
 9 The idea of excluding the parent from the education process.
10 Allowing parents to be actively involved and take part in teaching their own children at school.
11 She has difficulty choosing what to specialise in.
12 The original research Ruth would do for her doctorate, possibly involving exciting discoveries.
13 A period of maximum intellectual creativity in the development of the human mind.
14 The following points should be included:
    – as a five-year-old, Ruth already had the reading ability of a child of nine
    – she has just completed a three-year university course in two years at the age of thirteen
    – she covered seventeen topics in the last year, as opposed to the normal three or four
    – this enabled her to answer far more questions than those students normally classed as exceptional
    – she accumulated so many marks that if the next best student's total had been subtracted from hers she would still have gained a first-class degree easily
    – her average eight-hour daily work schedule has amazed even her university tutors
    – she is now preparing to study for a doctorate.

Use of English (p. 64)
A
 1 as/so   long
 2 term/concept/idea/phrase   impossible to define
    a difficult/impossible   term/concept/etc.   to define
 3 came from only/were made only   by
 4 the goal/aim/objective
 5 was/is   the
 6 but must/should/ought to   be
 7 will put them
 8 it is impossible/difficult
    teachers find impossible/difficult
 9 many/different/all   kinds/sorts/types   of
10 should/ought to/must   let ourselves be
    should/ought to/etc.   allow ourselves to be

B

1 She would still have had no trouble (in) getting/gaining   a First.
2 Ruth's Oxford tutors find her work astonishing.
3 Ruth's appetite for her subject cannot be satisfied.
  Ruth has an appetite for her subject which cannot be satisfied.
4 Mr Lawrence resigned from his job as a computer consultant.
5 He has a (very) low/poor/bad   opinion of the state educational system.
6 If it weren't/hadn't been   for a piece of legislation, they wouldn't have been there.
7 The expert advice of teachers could be beneficial to their children.
8 Some parents want to take (on) responsibility for their children's education.
9 They are both clearly excited by this idea.
  They both clearly find this idea exciting.
10 The creative period of the adult mind is over at 25.

Unit 11

Reading comprehension (p. 70)

T = True, F = False, ? = Don't know.
Section 1: 1 F   2 T   3 ?   4 T   5 F
Section 2: 1 ?   2 T   3 F   4 ?   5 ?
Section 3: 1 F   2 T   3 T   4 ?   5 T
Section 4: 1 T   2 F   3 T   4 ?   5 ?

Vocabulary
Section 1
1 supporters of the same team (Chelsea)
2 closely crowded/pressed together
3 the situation was serious/unpleasant
4 police with trained dogs
5 I met by chance and joined
6 strange-looking; bizarre in appearance
7 cut very short
8 thin straps (often elastic) passing over the shoulders used to hold up trousers

Section 2
9 attacking player
10 unrolled; opened out
11 surrounded by the enemy/hostile people
12 frequent/habitual customers
13 retaliation
14 worthless people; the lowest form of humanity
15 throwing*
16 enclosed space in front of a building

Section 3
17 revolving gates (especially at the entrances to sports stadiums) which admit only one person at a time
18 the fans' clothes were checked thoroughly to see if they were carrying weapons
19 the quantity of illegal objects found and confiscated (in this context)
20 groups with extreme/inflexible   opinions/attitudes
21 provoked verbally
22 organised/planned   fights/brawls (usually in large numbers)

23 separated; isolated

Section 4
24 jobs which don't involve manual work (e.g. bank/office jobs)
25 provoking verbally; taunting
26 fat stomachs (the result of habitual beer-drinking)
27 hanging loosely; spilling
28 provoking; encouraging; urging
29 provoke; encourge; urge
30 joyfully
31 painted crudely; smeared
32 run around out of control (often causing damage or injury)
33 stealing (from shops or private property whose windows/doors have been broken)
34 happens quickly and unexpectedly
35 hooligans; brutal people
36 attack
37 rapid, continuous number (of shots, kicks, blows, etc.)
38 boasting; praising oneself
39 began to; looked as if (he was) about to
40 cried; wept

Use of English (p. 73)

A

1	to	11	They
2	the	12	with/by
3	disguising/dressing	13	earned/won/gained
4	wearing	14	possibly/probably
5	match/game	15	totally/only/just/merely/solely
6	out	16	taken/got
7	in	17	over/around/round
8	battles/fights/confrontations/ skirmishes/attacks	18	on
9	that	19	else
10	to/against	20	enjoy/love

B

1 In spite of the fact that we were packed as tight as sardines into a football excursion train, the trip was quiet.
   In spite of being packed as tight as sardines into a football excursion train, the trip was quiet.
2 Not until they were safely among their own kind did they display/show/ reveal their scarves.
3 There was nobody/no-one (to be seen) in/on (the) streets on the way to the Watford ground.
4 I've seen no-one/none/nobody as bad as Stoke, Chelsea and West Ham (supporters).
   I've seen no-one/none/etc. as bad as those from Stoke, Chelsea and West Ham.
5 When they had gone through the turnstiles, the fans were body-searched for weapons.
6 Football probably has/holds no interest for him.
   Football probably doesn't interest him.

7　The reason (why) such battles are rare is because policing of the grounds has become more successful.
8　It would be wrong to say/think　that all football hooligans are unintelligent.
　　It would not be true/be untrue　to say that all football hooligans are unintelligent.
9　All he got/received　(as a reward) was a fusillade of kicks in the ribs.
10　The odds against him were eight to one.
　　The odds were eight to one against him.

Oral and written practice (p. 74)

Discussion topic (to the teacher)

If you feel that you don't have enough time for the role-play, or that it wouldn't fit in with your own plans, use the lead-in ideas (causes of and remedies for football hooliganism) as a basis for class discussion. If you do decide to do the role-play, some of the characters can be omitted, according to the number of students in each group　The character 'Marty Mckee' could be a man or a woman, depending on the male/female balance in each group.

Unit 12

Reading comprehension (p. 78)

First passage
1C　2D　3B　4B　5C

Second passage
6A　7B　8B　9D　10A

Use of English (p. 81)

A
1　I haven't had/touched/drunk　(any) booze for over a year.
　　I haven't been on the booze for over a year.
2　The increasing amount being spent on booze and advertising is what concerns me.
　　The thing that concerns me is the increasing amount being spent on booze and advertising.
3　What I did first was (to) head for the nearest pub.
4　The only effect/result　of a second trip to the same psycho ward was to make me more furtive.
5　I was in such a drunken state/condition　that I pushed by fist through the door.
　　I was in such a state of drunkenness that I pushed my fist through the door.
6　He had already been to a detoxification unit four times.
　　He had been to a detoxification unit four times before.
7　They'd told him, 'If you start to drink again, you won't last six months.'
8　Despite the fact that he was intelligent, he was in very bad shape both physically and mentally.
　　Despite being intelligent, he was in very bad shape both physically and mentally.
9　He wanted to know why they couldn't stop his nose bleeding.
10　No sooner had I begun to sober up than I began the 'hot and colds'.
　　No sooner did I begin to sober up than I began the 'hot and colds'.

B

1 the only way/needed	6 people being
2 an article	7 are on the
3 we ban it/it is banned	8 lead to/cause/produce a
4 born with/suffering from	9 a cure for/an answer to/thought about
5 or both (of its)	10 should/would be given

Unit 13

Reading comprehension (p. 84)

T = True, F = False, ? = Don't know.
Section 1: 1 T   2 T   3 F   4 T
Section 2: 1 ?   2 T   3 F   4 F
Section 3: 1 F   2 ?   3 T   4 ?
Section 4: 1 F   2 T   3 F   4 ?

Vocabulary
Section 1
1   a harmfully large amount of a drug taken at one time
2   highly unlikely
3   innocent; inexperienced
4   a change of opinion/philosophy
5   (the state of being) unemployed
6   a drug to relieve pain/dull the feelings (in this case drugs would help remove the pain/boredom   of everyday life)
7   a state of deep unconsciousness
8   cold and unwelcoming; desolate

Section 2
9   destroyed by fire
10   covered with boards (flat pieces of wood)
11   background; scene; setting
12   given prominence to; emphasised
13   a lot of (a score = 20)
14   a sudden increase
15   the drug arrived suddenly/dramatically   in Croxteth
16   became popular
17   a new fashion

Section 3
18   an official enquiry, usually into the cause of a death
19   died from
20   known to be true/factual
21   four-wheeled carriages for babies, pushed by hand
22   people who sell illegal drugs
23   with a barrier erected as a defence (in this case against the police) or to stop people entering
24   sold/traded (illegally)
25   things which are very profitable/useful (in this case stories for the media)
26   (painfully) unable to choose between
27   extreme sorrow/distress

Section 4
28   the basic facts

29　defeating/winning against　the authorities and the conventions of society
30　experienced in dealing with the situations and possible dangers of life in big cities
31　clever
32　clear/visible　proof or evidence
33　places where large amounts of heroin are sold illegally
34　very big; enormous

Use of English (p. 86)

A

1	to	11	closely
2	so	12	has
3	throughout/around	13	sources
4	warned/said	14	like/especially/particularly
5	for/to	15	to
6	drug/heroin	16	of
7	well	17	penalty/punishment
8	see/regard	18	imprisonment
9	both	19	on
10	against	20	allow/permit/facilitate

B

1　There is hardly any hope that this will change things.
　　It is hardly likely/possible　that this will change things
2　Nobody but/except/other than　the brave or naive would dare predict a change of heart.
3　There has been a sudden escalation that most (people) find/consider inexplicable.
　　There has been a sudden escalation that most (people) regard (as being) inexplicable.
　　There has been a sudden escalation that is inexplicable to most (people).
4　I had hardly any idea what it was.
　　I had almost no idea what it was.
5　There are schoolchildren who/that spend their dinner money on 'smack'.
6　Both (of them) intend to continue/carry on/go on.
7　A sixteen-year-old says that he has been paid £45.
　　A sixteen-year-old says that he was paid £45.
8　Nothing as exciting as heroin has ever happened in Croxteth.
9　To him,/In his opinion,　Croxteth symbolises the political isolation of Liverpool.
　　As far as he is concerned, Croxteth symbolises the political isolation of Liverpool.
10　Croxteth's record as a heroin trafficking centre is not as bad as Birkenhead's/that of Birkenhead.

Unit 14

Reading comprehension (p. 90)

1D　2C　3C　4D　5A

Vocabulary

A

1 defendants
2 planted
3 prestigious
4 aiming
5 current
6 strip
7 dagger
8 witness
9 skill
10 desperate men

B

1 on trial; under suspicion
2 accusations
3 place
4 foundations; basic elements
5 proof
6 making; conducting
7 indicating guilt
8 legal argument used to fight against an accusation
9 minor/small-time criminals
10 discovered; seen

Use of English (p. 92)

A

1 A fingerprint can be moved from one spot and placed elsewhere.
2 An inquiry into fingerprinting is being carried out by a committee of criminal lawyers.
3 By using/means of a strip of adhesive, a fingerprint can be 'lifted'.
4 It is nine years since these accusations were first made.
5 It used to be the custom/normal practice to show the object on which the prints were found.
   It used to be customary/normal to show the object on which the prints were found.
6 In spite of this line of defence failing/having failed in Britain, there have been two successful claims in the United States.
   In spite of the fact that this line of defence has failed in Britain, there have been two successful claims in the United States.
   In spite of there having been two successful claims in the United States, this line of defence has failed in Britain.
   In spite of the fact that there have been two successful claims in the United States, this line of defence has failed in Britain.
7 The truth of the allegations has not been proved.
   The truth of the allegations cannot be proved.
8 The police are always being accused by petty crooks of lifting their prints.
9 The new line of defence is seen by Mr Squires as an attack on the police by desperate men.
10 The method he would like to be/see generally used again is the old one.

B

1 A fingerprint can be moved.
2 Justice is a legal organisation which/that has/enjoys a good reputation.

Justice is a legal organisation with a good reputation.
3 A report should come out early next year.
A report is supposed/expected to come out early next year.
4 It is not our intention to establish if these allegations are true or not.
5 There is (some) anxiety among some of Britain's top criminal lawyers about this increasing number of claims.
6 The first time these accusations were made was nine years ago.
7 The law no longer insists on/demands/requires this.
This is no longer required by law.
8 This line of defence has had/met with no success in Britain.
This line of defence has not had/met with any success in Britain.
9 Lifting a mark and transferring it calls for great skill and trouble.
10 In Mr Squires' opinion, the new line of defence is an attack on the police.

Oral and written practice

Picture discussion
Possible explanatory sentences:
Adhesive tape is then pressed onto the print.
The tape is now peeled/pulled off, lifting the fingerprint.
The tape is then applied to another surface.
The tape is taken off, leaving a (clear) (finger)print.

Unit 15

Reading comprehension (p. 95)

Correct sequence: **b c e a d**

Vocabulary
a
1 targets
2 make off with
3 monitor
4 (tricky) sleights of hand
5 till

b
1 wailing
2 flopping out of
3 pregnant
4 indignity
5 squashed
6 knuckles
7 gripped
8 picked up
9 spotted
10 pinching

c
1 lifting
2 fumbled for words
3 tatty
4 impeccable credentials
5 baffled

d
1 stuffing
2 making for
3 keeled over
4 hypothermia
5 risk

e
1 discharge
2 vexed
3 on the spot
4 thieving (l 26); filching (l 39)
5 stiff

Use of English (p. 97)

A

1	in	11	someone/somebody
2	ready/about/intending	12	might/say
3	over/to/past	13	goods/clothes/gear/coats
4	checked	14	some
5	sense	15	so
6	among(st)	16	where
7	price	17	over
8	started/began	18	off
9	seemed/appeared	19	need/have
10	even	20	shoplifter/thief

B

1 heard/could hear   was the
2 item/coat   had been (hanging)
3 and then it; one moment, the next it
4 have learned (the trick)/have had lessons
5 as if/like   she could
6 the girl/thief/shoplifter   jumped
7 selling tickets; what he was doing
8 with the other
9 go (of) the
10 (that) she could give

Unit 16

Reading comprehension (p. 104)

1A   2D   3D   4C   5C

Vocabulary

A

1 a rise
2 fobbed off with
3 speak out
4 laid down
5 bribes
6 subservience
7 paternalism
8 immutable
9 bring about
10 pits
11 poach
12 reasserted themselves
13 harnessed
14 immune
15 repercussions

B

1 unconvincing/unsatisfactory   reason
2 forever; indefinitely; until you are exhausted
3 are serious
4 loyal to the Duke
5 stories/rumours   spread quickly
6 nothing in reserve; no possibility of bargaining
7 be dismissed; lose one's job
8 continuous efforts/attempts   over a long period of time
9 the normal situation
10 with political objectives; for political purposes

Use of English (p. 106)

A

1	ago	11	factory
2	out	12	whole
3	like	13	suit/fit
4	let	14	for
5	felt/was	15	worth
6	all	16	Suppose/Imagine
7	found/got	17	employed
8	concluded/decided	18	After/Following
9	enough	19	come/be
10	mine/pit	20	return

B

1 It's years since they were first promised a rise.
   They were first promised a rise years ago.
2 The estate hasn't/doesn't have   enough money to pay them.
3 He was the first to speak out openly in support of the beaters.
4 Strikes did not belong to his world.
5 Henry felt that just working/to work   for them was a privilege.
   Henry felt that it was a privilege just working/to work   for them.
6 On top of his minimum wage, he was paid an extra £5 a week for his position as Head keeper.
7 It took one minor bribe after another to get repairs done.
8 Paternalism and social inequality could not be changed.
9 They had poached the Duke's land prior to becoming gamekeepers.
10 The repercussions would affect even the Duke.

Unit 17 (p. 109)

Reading comprehension

Suggested answers.
1 The way in which the structure of society is becoming more and more complex and disorderly.
2 Treating the physical symptoms as if they are the problem itself, without searching for the real causes.
   Trying to pretend there are no symptoms and that therefore there is no problem.
3 A cut of the surgeon's knife; or more figuratively, removing the tumour of incompetence by surgical means.
4 Because most people are selfish and only interested in their own problems, not other people's.
5 The Final Placement Syndrome patients.
6 He has reached the level beyond which he will not advance in his profession.
7 It would mean giving up the only pleasures he still has; he would not be willing to do that, as the only alternative, work, is not giving him any pleasure. These pleasures might also give him a sense of worth, and giving them up might entail a loss of self-esteem.
8 Because they can find nothing physically wrong with the patient.
9 Because it represents what the patient himself says or thinks, even though this might not actually be true.

10 Phoney/fake doctors; charlatans; people who claim to have medical expertise, but who are not qualified doctors.
11 'Copelessness' means the inability to do, or deal with, his job properly. 'Something that he can cope with' means something that he can do reasonably well.
12 The following points should be mentioned:
    – some doctors attack the physical symptoms with medication or surgery.
    – advice to relax and work less is given
    – the philosophical approach: everyone has problems; it is natural for the patient to have problems at his age
    – threats are made: the patient will finish up in hospital or have serious health problems in the future
    – self-denial is recommended: diet, drink and smoke less, give up night-life, have less sex
    – some doctors try to persuade the patient that there is nothing wrong with him
    – even psychotherapy is tried, if the above things fail
    – distraction therapy, which encourages the patient to take up a new hobby, is the only treatment which helps.

Use of English (p. 111)

A

1	among(st)/for	11	If
2	ask/request/demand	12	idea/concept/precept
3	down	13	which
4	adage/saying	14	locked/closed
5	to	15	business
6	be	16	those/people
7	further/develop/help	17	cannot
8	other	18	bear
9	own	19	on/upon
10	on/upon	20	competitors/adversaries

B
1 The medical profession has failed to recognize that the Final Placement Syndrome exists.
2 They claim that their physical ailments cause/are the cause of their occupational incompetence.
3 You're not in a worse position than lots of other people.
  Your position is no worse than that of lots of other people.
  Your position is no worse than lots of other people's.
4 They don't show much interest in philosophy.
5 Cut down on food.
6 This advice doesn't usually work.
7 He won't feel like giving it up.
8 These symptoms are only a figment of his/your/one's/the imagination.
9 There is a chance (that) he will lose faith altogether in orthodox medicine.
10 Take up stamp collecting/collecting stamps.

Unit 18

Reading comprehension (p. 115)

T = True, F = False, ? = Don't know

First passage

1T   2F   3?   4?   5?   6T

Second passage

7?   8T   9T   10?   11F   12T

Vocabulary

A

1   suggested; put forward for consideration
2   trying to achieve a particular aim, through a series of planned activities
3   remove completely; eliminate
4   prejudice
5   small child who has just learnt to walk
6   an experimental project
7   I'm completely in favour of
8   useful
9   occupy oneself pleasantly
10 Have you ever heard anything more stupid?*
11 confused
12 had the principal role
13 a traditional Christmas show for children, based on a fairy-tale, with music, dancing and clowning.
14 scratched/scraped with rapid movements of the hands
15 without a point or an edge (usually used for knives, but in this case it probably means 'without claws')
16 feet (of certain animals)
17 looked (at something) with half-closed eyes
18 play roughly and noisily
19 walking/moving with style and energy
20 in women's clothing

B

1   womb
2   subjected
3   assertiveness
4   seeking
5   forfeiting
6   intrinsic
7   distorting/perverting
8   propped
9   capering around
10 upsurge

Use of English (p. 117)

A

1   possible/feasible/realistic
2   either
3   any/a
4   less
5   in/when
6   to
7   which/that
8   gain
9   superiority/supremacy
10 greater/natural
11 treated
12 of
13 opportunity/chance
14 few
15 only
16 equal/rival
17 should
18 need
19 activities/occupations
20 which

B

1 Some of them seem/appear   to be campaigning for 'role reversal'.
2 I've got nothing against that idea.
3 Have you (ever) heard (of) anything as daft as/dafter than   that?
4 It took us quite a while to persuade him to play in the garden.
5 I hope that relating to his early kindergarten life was not why/the reason   he went mining.
6 The difference between men and women is explained in a book I've been reading.
7 Had it been a boy, it would have been subjected to another chemical.
8 Despite the fact that they might be like my daughter, it's not a creative kind of assertiveness.
  Despite the possibility that they are like my daughter, it's not a creative kind of assertiveness.
  Despite (the possibility of) their/them   being like my daughter, it's not a creative kind of assertiveness.
9 Not only are these women wasting their time, but (they are) also forfeiting their intrinsic nature.
10 It's a pity I didn't change its nappy.

Unit 19

Reading comprehension (p. 122)

Correct sequence: **d   a   c   e   b**

Vocabulary

a
1 harden themselves (mentally)
2 not give up until something (unpleasant) is completed
3 an impractical idea; a fantasy
4 be badly beaten physically; be brutally attacked
5 recover consciousness
6 discolorations on the skin caused by a blow or knock
7 is not what they want or like
8 shoes with high heels (the 'heel' is the raised part of the back of the shoe)
9 people acting the part of attackers
10 unwilling

b
1 hit/strike hard
2 held out; extended
3 break*
4 attacker
5 move carefully and slowly . . . round
6 turning; twisting
7 hit violently*
8 someone who can be attacked easily (in this context)
9 improve one's physical fitness
10 people who attack those who are weaker than themselves

c
1 initial physical exercise (before a game, match or more intense activity)
2 mixture of
3 a type of comedy depending on physical actions (e.g. as practised by circus clowns)

4 lose balance; stumble
  5 a dull sound (as of a soft body falling on a harder surface)
  6 ironical
  7 secure; position firmly
  8 weak; fragile
  9 weak; ineffectual
 10 kind; gentle

d
  1 surrender/submit to; accept without resistance
  2 pull/rip from
  3 opposed; blocked; resisted
  4 unbeatable
  5 use . . . against him
  6 submit; give in
  7 great physical size
  8 rigid bars used as tools to move or lift things more easily
  9 skilful; clever; crafty
 10 Fight with disregard for the accepted rules

e
  1 blow*
  2 bone to which one's teeth are attached
  3 narrow street/passage   between buildings
  4 doesn't stay in your memory
  5 blow (with the fist)

Use of English (p. 125)

A
  1 I'd like to know how many of them have learned how to fight.
  2 Women don't like hitting/to hit   each other hard enough.
  3 8 lbs of pressure is enough/sufficient/all it needs   to break an elbow.
     8 lbs of pressure will/would   be sufficient/enough   to break an elbow.
  4 Describing it is much harder/more difficult/more complicated   than doing
     it.
  5 Women may have been made something of an easy touch by years of
     conditioning.
  6 In spite of ending up free, you'll be bald.
     In spite of the fact that you'll end up free, you'll be bald.
  7 There is no other system of self-defence for women like/to compare with   it.
  8 Though women have a different build, they (still) have advantages over
     men.
     Though women are built differently, they (still) have advantages over men.
  9 'I feel more confident now that I have learned self-defence,' she said.
 10 Simple principles form/compose/are   the basis of the Biffen method.
     Simple principles are what the Biffen method is based on/consists of.

B
  1 Look on/upon   it as a competition of minds.
  2 When I won, I didn't feel (any pain from) the bruises.
  3 The Biffen method is supposed to work however you dress.
  4 He would like more women to get in trim.
  5 Biffen makes it harder/more difficult   to forget with a wry commentary.
  6 I'm not going to use an imitation knife.

7   There is no reason why you should knuckle under to male violence when you can tear off his ear.
8   It takes no/doesn't take any   more strength than folding the Guardian in half.
9   Bulk is/becomes   unnecessary if you can use your limbs as levers.
10 Some ideas seem such obvious ones that it is surprising most women are unaware of them.
    It is surprising (that) most women are unaware of such obvious ideas.

Unit 20

Reading comprehension (p. 128)

1B   2A   3C   4A   5D

Vocabulary
1   loops of thread to sew up a wound
2   reflecting; considering it carefully
3   insane/mad
4   deceived; misled; suffering from delusions
5   lunatic (possibly behaving violently or talking nonsense)
6   It's obvious what impression that gives of me
7   selfish/egotistical
8   put in prison (or in this case a mental institution)
9   make you suffer*
10 Is that what I wanted?*
11 such a big lie
12 I won't accept it*
13 I'm going*
14 I'm certainly not staying here*
15 in no condition to travel
16 they can contact me at my mother's house*
17 that's typical of you
18 an insulting term for someone who is despicable, servile or flatters people to impress.*
19 vulgar/unrefined   behaviour at mealtimes
20 heavy drinking (of alcohol)*
21 awful friends
22 awful/terrible
23 You've no social manners (because you're from a lower social class)
24 and that's all; no more than that*
25 crazy/mad/insane*

Use of English (p. 130)

A
1   you've had
2   must have
3   whether/if they're
4   not only feel/think/believe
5   not/never   to do it
6   According to a/some
7   to be more/would be more
8   (actually) hits/assaults/batters   his
9   has been doing
10 happens to

B
1   You think I inflicted that cut on myself.

172

2   I didn't know what to think.
3   You take someone else's word rather than your wife's/what your wife
     tells you.
     You take the word of someone else rather than your wife's/what your
     wife tells you.
4   I realised that this was a question without an answer.
5   You're in no state to travel, you need rest.
     You're not in a/any   state to travel, you need rest.
6   Don't bother to try me there yourself.
7   Your lack of respect for women is due to (your) lack of breeding.
     Your having no respect for women is due to (your) having no breeding.
8   There's no point (in) taking anything they say seriously.
     What's the point (of) taking anything they say seriously?
9   You believe him in spite of his/him being out of his mind.
10   I only wish I'd found out about you sooner.
     If only I'd found out about you sooner.

Answer Key to Tests

Test One

1) B	11) B	21) C	31) B	41) A
2) C	12) C	22) D	32) C	42) C
3) B	13) D	23) C	33) A	43) B
4) D	14) A	24) D	34) A	44) D
5) D	15) B	25) D	35) A	45) D
6) C	16) A	26) B	36) C	46) A
7) A	17) D	27) B	37) B	47) D
8) A	18) B	28) A	38) A	48) A
9) A	19) A	29) C	39) B	49) B
10) D	20) A	30) D	40) D	50) C

Test Two

1) C	11) B	21) A	31) C	41) C
2) C	12) D	22) A	32) A	42) D
3) A	13) A	23) B	33) D	43) B
4) C	14) B	24) B	34) B	44) D
5) A	15) D	25) A	35) B	45) A
6) B	16) C	26) D	36) C	46) D
7) A	17) D	27) C	37) B	47) C
8) D	18) A	28) C	38) B	48) B
9) B	19) A	29) B	39) B	49) A
10) D	20) A	30) C	40) D	50) B

Test Three

1) A	11) C	21) D	31) D	41) D
2) C	12) A	22) A	32) A	42) B
3) B	13) A	23) B	33) C	43) B
4) A	14) A	24) A	34) B	44) A
5) D	15) C	25) A	35) C	45) B
6) D	16) C	26) D	36) C	46) C
7) A	17) C	27) D	37) B	47) D
8) D	18) B	28) C	38) A	48) D
9) B	19) D	29) B	39) C	49) A
10) A	20) A	30) C	40) A	50) C

Test Four

1) B	11) C	21) B	31) A	41) D
2) C	12) C	22) A	32) B	42) C
3) A	13) B	23) B	33) A	43) A
4) C	14) A	24) D	34) B	44) B
5) B	15) A	25) D	35) D	45) C
6) D	16) B	26) D	36) C	46) C
7) D	17) D	27) B	37) C	47) A
8) A	18) C	28) B	38) D	48) B
9) A	19) B	29) C	39) A	49) B
10) C	20) C	30) B	40) D	50) B

Acknowledgements

The publishers would like to thank the following for permission to reproduce copyright material. They have tried to contact all copyright holders, but in cases where they may have failed will be pleased to make the necessary arrangements at the first opportunity.

André Deutsch Ltd for the extract from *Switzerland for Beginners* by George Mikes, published by André Deutsch Ltd, 1975 (page 9);

Central Office of Information for their anti-heroin campaign poster (page 88);

Century Hutchinson Publishing Group Ltd for the extracts from *Stanley and the Women* by Kingsley Amis (pages 128 and 130);

Dr. Ivor K. Davies for the extracts from *The Management of Learning* published by McGraw-Hill, 1971 (pages 57 and 59);

English Speaking Board (International) Ltd for the extract from a report in *Spoken English Magazine (vol 15, no. 3)* on an address by Harry Armstrong in July 1982 (page 64);

Express Newspapers plc for the articles and extracts from the *Daily Express*: 'The Finger of Suspicion' (page 90) and from the *Sunday Express*: 'One Way to Look at an Overdraft' (page 136), 'Happiness Worth a Million' (pages 136, 138, 140, 142, 144, 145), 'The Unteachables, by a Headmaster' (page 53), 'Top Red Calls on Russia to Ban the Bottle' (page 82), 'Will Those Small Boys Ever Get Over It?' (page 115) and the article on Cline and Spender (page 145);

Sharon Feinstein for the article 'Okay Yah!' (page 16);

Gingerbread for their advertisement on page 137;

Greenwich Action Committee Against Racist Attacks for their advertisement (page 143);

The Guardian for the article 'Seven Days that Led to a Year on the Wagon' (pages 78 and 80);

Hereford and Worcester Probation Service for their advertisement (page 136);

London News Service for articles from the *News of the World*: '£85,000 in a Day for Joan!' (page 30), 'Storm over Selina's Pay' (page 30), 'Sir Isn't Pleased with Classroom Capers' (page 50) and 'Find That George Best Orders Court' (page 141);

Longman Group for the extract from chapter 25 of *For and Against* by L. G. Alexander (page 13);

Mail Newspapers plc for the extracts and articles from the *Daily Mail*: 'The Game of Tennis is under Threat from the Mini-brat' (page 38), 'It's a Steal in the Big City Jungle' (page 97) and from the *Mail on Sunday*—'For Love and Money' (page 40);

McGraw-Hill Book Company for the table from *The Human Side of Enterprise* by D. McGregor published by McGraw-Hill, 1960 (page 56);

Michael Joseph Ltd for extracts from *The Gamekeeper* by B. Hines, published, by Michael Joseph Ltd (pages 21, 48(c), 49(d) and 104);

North West London Housing Association for their advertisement (page 142);

The Observer for the extracts and articles 'Queen of Hearts' (page 7), 'Business as Usual in Smack City' (page 84), 'London Shops Brace for 16 Thieving Days' (page 95), and 'Moving Up' (page 138);

Penguin Books Ltd for the extracts from *Human Aggression* by Anthony Storr published by Penguin Books, 1968 (pages 12 and 117) and the extract from *Connexions:Work* by Colin Ward published by Penguin Educational, 1972 (page 106);

Private Eye for the extracts from the 'Wimmin' column (page 120);

Quartet Books Ltd for the extract from *My Queen and I* by W. Hamilton (page 8);

Angela Singer for the article 'How Are the Mighty Fallen' (page 122);

David Storey for the extract from *Present Times* (page 116);
Syndication International Ltd for extracts and articles from the *Daily Mirror*: 'Arab pays £95,000 for Picnic' (page 140), 'Are they the Wild Ones?' (page 54) and quotes from an article on education (page 54);
from the *Sunday Mirror*: 'The Rich Kids' (pages 24 and 26), 'Miss Cannon is no Snip' (page 140), 'Rent-a-Royal Cash Fury' (page 29), 'Clough the Defender' (page 43), 'The Hunters and the Hunted' (pages 46 and 48(a)), 'Saturday, Bloody Saturday' (pages 70 and 73), 'Men get the Needle' (page 120), 'Best Beats the Booze—Amazing Drink Cure' (page 139);
and from the *Sunday People*: 'Hooligans on Horseback' (page 48 (b));
Tribune de Genève for the advertisement for a butler (page 137);
Unigate Dairies Ltd for their advertisement (page 137);
The Washington Post for the extract from 'Drug War: British Seek Right Language' (page 86);
Wigan Metropolitan Borough Council for their advertisement (page 143);
William Morrow and Co. for the passage excerpted from *The Peter Principle* by Dr. Laurence J. Peter and Raymond Hull published by William Morrow and Co., 1969 (page 109);
E. K. Winterbottom for the letter 'Ban the Cane and Give Freedom to the Bully Boys?' (page 52);
Yorkshire Post for the extract from the article 'Good brain + hard work = "genius" ' (page 62).

The publishers are grateful to the following for permission to reproduce illustrations and photographs:

Illustrations
Express Newspapers plc (page 94, from the *Daily Express*); London News Service (page 47, from the *News of the World*); *Private Eye* (page 83); Pierre Reymond (page 10); Paul Slater (page 15); Syndication International (page 132, from the *Sunday Mirror*).

Photographs
All Sport, Tony Duff (page 119); Associated Press Photos (page 42); Ed Barber (page 99); BBC Hulton Library (page 28); Sally and Richard Greenhill (page 60); Network, John Sturrock (page 108); LWT (page 34); Sporting Pictures UK Ltd (page 75); Syndication International (page 22); Wang (UK) Ltd (page 113).